BRITISH RAILW

LOCO

CU00660307

FIFTY-THIRD EDITION
2011

The Complete Guide to all
Locomotives which operate on
the national railway network
and Eurotunnel

Robert Pritchard & Peter Fox

ISBN 978 1902 336 79 4

© 2010. Platform 5 Publishing Ltd., 3 Wyvern House, Sark Road, Sheffield, S2 4HG, England.

Printed in England by Information Press, Eynsham, Oxford.

CONTENTS

PROVISION OF INFORMATION

This book has been compiled with care to be as accurate as possible, but in some cases information is not officially available and the publisher cannot be held responsible for any errors or omissions. We would like to thank the companies and individuals which have been co-operative in supplying information to us. The authors of this series of books are always pleased to receive notification from readers of any inaccuracies readers may find in the series, to enhance future editions. Please send comments to:

Robert Pritchard, Platform 5 Publishing Ltd., 3 Wyvern House, Sark Road, Sheffield, S2 4HG, England.

e-mail: <u>robert@platform5.com</u>   **Tel:** 0114 255 2625   **Fax:** 0114 255 2471

This book is updated to information received by 4 October 2010.

UPDATES

This book is updated to the Stock Changes given in **Today's Railways UK 107** (November 2010). Readers are therefore advised to update this book from the official Platform 5 Stock Changes published every month in **Today's Railways UK** magazine, starting with issue 108.

The Platform 5 magazine **Today's Railways UK** contains news and rolling stock information on the railways of Britain and Ireland and is published on the second Monday of every month.

Front cover photograph: Stobart Rail-liveried 92017 "Bart the Engine" powers through Docker with 4S43 06.22 Rugby–Mossend Tesco intermodal on 20/04/10.
Tom Mcatee

BRITAIN'S RAILWAY SYSTEM

INFRASTRUCTURE & OPERATION

Britain's national railway infrastructure is owned by a "not for dividend" company, Network Rail. Many stations and maintenance depots are leased to and operated by Train Operating Companies (TOCs), but some larger stations remain under Network Rail control. The only exception is the infrastructure on the Isle of Wight, which is nationally owned and is leased to South West Trains.

Trains are operated by TOCs over Network Rail, regulated by access agreements between the parties involved. In general, TOCs are responsible for the provision and maintenance of the locos, rolling stock and staff necessary for the direct operation of services, whilst NR is responsible for the provision and maintenance of the infrastructure and also for staff to regulate the operation of services.

DOMESTIC PASSENGER TRAIN OPERATORS

The large majority of passenger trains are operated by the TOCs on fixed term franchises. Franchise expiry dates are shown in the list of franchisees below:

Franchise	Franchisee	Trading Name
Chiltern Railways	Deutsche Bahn (until 31 December 2021)	Chiltern Railways
Cross-Country[1]	Deutsche Bahn (Arriva) (until 1 November 2013)	CrossCountry
East Midlands[2]	Stagecoach Holdings plc (until 11 November 2013)	East Midlands Trains
Greater Western[3]	First Group plc (until 1 April 2013)	First Great Western
Greater Anglia	National Express Group plc (until 14 October 2011)	National Express East Anglia
Integrated Kent[4]	GoVia Ltd. (Go-Ahead/Keolis) (until 3 March 2012)	Southeastern
InterCity East Coast[5]		East Coast
InterCity West Coast	Virgin Rail Group Ltd. (until 31 March 2012)	Virgin Trains
London Rail[6]	MTR/Deutsche Bahn (until 14 March 2014)	London Overground
LTS Rail[7]	National Express Group plc (until further notice)	c2c
Merseyrail Electrics[8]	Serco/NedRail (until 20 July 2028)	Merseyrail
Northern Rail	Serco/Abellio (until 15 September 2013)	Northern
ScotRail	First Group plc (until 8 November 2014)	ScotRail
South Central[9]	GoVia Ltd. (Go-Ahead/Keolis) (until 25 July 2015)	Southern

South Western[10]	Stagecoach Holdings plc (until 4 February 2014)	South West Trains
Thameslink/Great Northern[11]	First Group plc (until 1 April 2012)	First Capital Connect
Trans-Pennine Express[12]	First Group/Keolis (until 1 February 2012)	TransPennine Express
Wales & Borders	Deutsche Bahn (Arriva) (until 6 December 2018)	Arriva Trains Wales
West Midlands[13]	GoVia Ltd. (Go-Ahead/Keolis) (until 19 September 2013)	London Midland

Notes:

[1] Awarded for six years to 2013 with an extension for a further two years and five months to 1 April 2016 if performance targets are met.

[2] Awarded for six years to 2013 with an extension for a further one year and five months to 1 April 2015 if performance targets are met.

[3] Awarded for seven years to 2013 with an extension for a further three years to 1 April 2016 if performance targets are met.

[4] The Integrated Kent franchise started on 1 April 2006 for an initial period of six years to 2012, with an extension for a further two years to 1 April 2014 if performance targets are met.

[5] Currently run on an interim basis by DfT management company Directly Operated Railways (trading as East Coast) following financial difficulties experienced by National Express Group.

[6] The London Rail Concession is different from all other rail franchises, as fares and service levels are set by Transport for London instead of the DfT. Incorporates the North and West London lines, the Gospel Oak–Barking line and Euston–Watford local services.

[7] Tendering for the new LTS Rail franchise, to be called Essex Thameside, has been delayed whilst the Government conducts a consultation exercise on the future of rail franchising policy (the franchise has been due to finish on 25 May 2011). The Greater Anglia franchise has also been given a short extension for the same reason.

[8] Now under control of Merseytravel PTE instead of the DfT. Franchise due to be reviewed after seven years (in July 2010) and then every five years to fit in with the Merseyside Local Transport Plan.

[9] Awarded for five years and ten months to 2015 with a possible extension for a further two years to 25 July 2017.

[10] Awarded for seven years to 2014 with an extension for a further three years to 4 February 2017 if performance targets are met.

[11] Awarded for six years to 2012 with an extension for up to a further three years to 1 April 2015 if performance targets are met.

[12] Awarded for eight years to 2012 with an extension a further five years to 1 February 2017 if performance targets are met.

[13] Awarded for six years to 2013 with an extension for a further two years to 19 September 2015 if performance targets are met.

All new franchises officially start at 02.00 on the first day. Because of this the finishing date of an old franchise and the start date of its successor are the same.

Where termination dates are dependent on performance targets being met, the earliest possible termination date is given. However, with Merseyrail the termination date is based on the maximum franchise length.

The following operators run non-franchised services only:

Operator	Trading Name	Route
BAA	Heathrow Express	London Paddington–Heathrow Airport
First Hull Trains	First Hull Trains	London King's Cross–Hull
Grand Central	Grand Central	London King's Cross–Sunderland/ Bradford Interchange
North Yorkshire Moors Railway Enterprises	North Yorkshire Moors Railway	Pickering–Grosmont–Whitby/ Battersby
West Coast Railway Company	West Coast Railway Company	Birmingham–Stratford-upon-Avon Fort William–Mallaig* York–Leeds–York–Scarborough* Machynlleth–Porthmadog/Pwllheli*
Wrexham, Shropshire & Marylebone Railway	Wrexham & Shropshire	London Marylebone–Wrexham General

* Special summer-dated services only.

INTERNATIONAL PASSENGER OPERATIONS

Eurostar (UK) operates passenger services between the UK and mainland Europe, jointly with the national operators of France (SNCF) and Belgium (SNCB/NMBS). Eurostar (UK) is a subsidiary of London & Continental Railways, which is jointly owned by National Express Group and British Airways.

In addition, a service for the conveyance of accompanied road vehicles through the Channel Tunnel is provided by the tunnel operating company, Eurotunnel.

FREIGHT TRAIN OPERATIONS

The following operators operate freight services or empty passenger stock workings under "Open Access" arrangements:

Colas Rail
DB Schenker Rail (UK)
Direct Rail Services (DRS)
Europorte2 (Eurotunnel)
Freightliner
GB Railfreight (owned by Eurotunnel)
West Coast Railway Company

INTRODUCTION

SCOPE

This section contains details of all locomotives which can run on Britain's national railway network, plus those of Eurotunnel. Locomotives which are owned by, for example, DB Schenker and Freightliner which have been withdrawn from service and awaiting disposal are listed in the main part of the book. Locos which are awaiting disposal at scrapyards are listed in the "Locomotives Awaiting Disposal" section.

Only preserved locomotives which are currently used on the National Rail network are included. Others, which may be Network Rail registered but not at present certified for use, are not included, but will be found in the new thirteenth edition of the Platform 5 book, "Preserved Locomotives & Multiple Units" (due to be published December 2009).

LOCO CLASSES

Loco classes are listed in numerical order of class. Principal details and dimensions are quoted for each class in metric and/or imperial units as considered appropriate bearing in mind common UK usage.

All dimensions and weights are quoted for locomotives in an "as new" condition with all necessary supplies (e.g. oil, water and sand) on board. Dimensions are quoted in the order length x width. Lengths quoted are over buffers or couplers as appropriate. All widths quoted are maxima. Where two different wheel diameter dimensions are shown, the first refers to powered wheels and the second refers to non-powered wheels.

NUMERICAL LISTINGS

Locomotives are listed in numerical order. Where numbers actually carried are different from those officially allocated, these are noted in class headings where appropriate. Where locomotives have been recently renumbered, the most immediate previous number is shown in parentheses. Each locomotive entry is laid out as in the following example:

RSL No. Detail Livery Owner Pool   Allocn.   Name

57302 d   **VT**   P   IWCA   MA   VIRGIL TRACY

Detail Differences. Only detail differences which currently affect the areas and types of train which locomotives may work are shown. All other detail differences are specifically excluded. Where such differences occur within a class or part class, they are shown in the "Detail" column alongside the individual locomotive number.

Standard abbreviations used are:

a	Train air brake equipment only.
b	Drophead buckeye couplers.
c	Scharfenberg couplers.
d	Fitted with retractable Dellner couplers.
e	European Railway Traffic Management System (ERTMS) signalling equipment fitted.
k	Fitted with Swinghead Automatic "buckeye" combination couplers.
p	Train air, vacuum and electro-pneumatic brakes.
r	Radio Electric Token Block (RETB) signalling equipment fitted
s	Slow Speed Control equipment.
v	Train vacuum brake only.
x	Train air and vacuum brakes ("Dual brakes").
+	Additional fuel tank capacity.
§	Sandite laying equipment.

In all cases use of the above abbreviations indicates the equipment indicated is normally operable. Meaning of non-standard abbreviations and symbols is detailed in individual class headings.

Codes. Codes are used to denote the livery, owner, pool and depot of each locomotive. Details of these will be found in section 7 of this book.

Names. Only names carried with official sanction are listed. Names are shown in UPPER/lower case characters as actually shown on the name carried on the locomotive.

GENERAL INFORMATION

CLASSIFICATION AND NUMBERING

All locomotives are classified and allocated numbers by the Rolling Stock Library under the TOPS numbering system, introduced in 1972. This comprises a two-digit class number followed by a three-digit serial number. Where the actual number carried by a locomotive differs from the allocated number, or where an additional number is carried to the allocated number, this is shown by a note in the class heading.

For diesel locomotives, class numbers offer an indication of engine horsepower as shown in the table below.

Class No. Range	Engine h.p.
01–14	0–799
15–20	800–1000
21–31	1001–1499
32–39	1500–1999
40–54, 57	2000–2999
55–56, 58–70	3000+

For electric locomotives class numbers are allocated in ascending numerical order under the following scheme:

| Class 71–80 | direct current and DC/diesel dual system locomotives. |
| Class 81 onwards | alternating current and AC/DC dual system locos. |

Numbers in the 89xxx series are allocated by the Rolling Stock Library to locomotives which have been de-registered but subsequently re-registered for use on the Network Rail network and whose original number has already been re-used. 89xxx numbers are normally only carried inside locomotive cabs and are not carried externally in normal circumstances.

WHEEL ARRANGEMENT

For main line locomotives the number of driven axles on a bogie or frame is denoted by a letter (A = 1, B = 2, C = 3 etc.) and the number of non-powered axles is denoted by a number. The use of the letter "o" after a letter indicates each axle is individually powered, whilst the "+" symbol indicates bogies are inter-coupled.

For shunting locomotives, the Whyte notation is used. In this notation the number of leading wheels are given, followed by the number of driving wheels and then the trailing wheels.

HAULAGE CAPABILITY OF DIESEL LOCOMOTIVES

The haulage capability of a diesel locomotive depends upon three basic factors:

1. Adhesive weight. The greater the weight on the driving wheels, the greater the adhesion and more tractive power can be applied before wheelslip occurs.

2. The characteristics of its transmission. To start a train the locomotive has to exert a pull at standstill. A direct drive diesel engine cannot do this, hence the need for transmission. This may be mechanical, hydraulic or electric. The present British Standard for locomotives is electric transmission. Here the diesel engine drives a generator or alternator and the current produced is fed to the traction motors. The force produced by each driven wheel depends on the current in its traction motor. In other words, the larger the current, the harder it pulls. As the locomotive speed increases, the current in the traction motor falls, hence the *Maximum Tractive Effort* is the maximum force at its wheels the locomotive can exert at a standstill. The electrical equipment cannot take such high currents for long without overheating. Hence the *Continuous Tractive Effort* is quoted which represents the current which the equipment can take continuously.

3. The power of its engine. Not all power reaches the rail, as electrical machines are approximately 90% efficient. As the electrical energy passes through two such machines (the generator or alternator and the traction motors), the *Power at Rail* is approximately 81% (90% of 90%) of the engine power, less a further amount used for auxiliary equipment such as radiator fans, traction motor blowers, air compressors, battery charging, cab heating, Electric Train Supply (ETS) etc. The power of the locomotive is proportional to the tractive effort times the speed. Hence when on full power there is a speed corresponding to the continuous tractive effort.

HAULAGE CAPABILITY OF ELECTRIC LOCOMOTIVES

Unlike a diesel locomotive, an electric locomotive does not develop its power on board and its performance is determined only by two factors, namely its weight and the characteristics of its electrical equipment. Whereas a diesel locomotive tends to be a constant power machine, the power of an electric locomotive varies considerably. Up to a certain speed it can produce virtually a constant tractive effort. Hence power rises with speed according to the formula given in section three above, until a maximum speed is reached at which tractive effort falls, such that the power also falls. Hence the power at the speed corresponding to the maximum tractive effort is lower than the maximum speed.

BRAKE FORCE

The brake force is a measure of the braking power of a locomotive. This is shown on the locomotive data panels so operating staff can ensure sufficient brake power is available on freight trains.

ELECTRIC TRAIN SUPPLY (ETS)

A number of locomotives are equipped to provide a supply of electricity to the train being hauled to power auxiliaries such as heating, cooling fans, air conditioning and kitchen equipment. ETS is provided from the locomotive by means of a separate alternator (except Class 33 locos, which have a DC generator). The ETS index of a locomotive is a measure of the electrical power available for train supply.

Similarly, most loco-hauled coaches also have an ETS index, which in this case is a measure of the power required to operate equipment mounted in the coach. The sum of the ETS indices of all the hauled vehicles in a train must not exceed the ETS index of the locomotive.

ETS is commonly (but incorrectly) known as ETH (Electric Train Heating), which is a throwback to the days before loco-hauled coaches were equipped with electrically powered auxiliary equipment other than for train heating.

ROUTE AVAILABILITY (RA)

This is a measure of a railway vehicle's axle load. The higher the axle load of a vehicle, the higher the RA number on a scale from 1 to 10. Each Network Rail route has a RA number and in general no vehicle with a higher RA number may travel on that route without special clearance.

MULTIPLE & PUSH-PULL WORKING

Multiple working between vehicles (i.e. two or more powered vehicles being driven from one cab) is facilitated by jumper cables connecting the vehicles. However, not all types are compatible with each other, and a number of different systems are in use, each system being incompatible with any other.

Association of American Railroads (AAR) System: Classes 59, 66, and 67.
Blue Star Coupling Code: Classes 20, 25, 31, 33, 37, 40 and 73.
DRS System: Classes 20/3, 37 and 47.
Green Circle Coupling Code: Class 47 (not all equipped).
Orange Square Coupling Code: Class 50.
Red Diamond Coupling Code: Classes 56 and 58.
SR System: Classes 33/1, 73 and various electric multiple units.
Within Own Class only: Classes 43, 60 and 70.

Many locomotives use a time-division multiplex (TDM) system for push-pull and multiple working which utilises the existing RCH jumper cables fitted to coaching stock vehicles. Previously these cables had only been used to control train lighting and public address systems.

Class 47 locos 47701–47717 were equipped with an older non-standard TDM system.

1. DIESEL LOCOMOTIVES

CLASS 08   BR/ENGLISH ELECTRIC   0-6-0

Built: 1955–1962 by BR at Crewe, Darlington, Derby Locomotive, Doncaster or Horwich Works.
Engine: English Electric 6KT of 298 kW (400 h.p.) at 680 r.p.m.
Main Generator: English Electric 801.
Traction Motors: Two English Electric 506.
Maximum Tractive Effort: 156 kN (35000 lbf).
Continuous Tractive Effort: 49 kN (11100 lbf) at 8.8 m.p.h.

Power At Rail: 194 kW (260 h.p.).	**Train Brakes:** Air & vacuum.
Brake Force: 19 t.	**Dimensions:** 8.92 x 2.59 m.
Weight: 49.6–50.4 t.	**Wheel Diameter:** 1372 mm.
Design Speed: 20 m.p.h.	**Maximum Speed:** 15 m.p.h.
Fuel Capacity: 3037 litres.	**RA:** 5.

Train Supply: Not equipped.
Multiple Working: m Equipped for multiple working. All others not equipped.

Notes: † – Fitted with remote control equipment.

Actual locations for all operational shunters are given, apart from DB Schenker and Freightliner-operated locos which generally move about on a more regular basis.

Certain Class 08s that don't have Network Rail engineering acceptance are classed as "in industrial service" and can be found in section 4 of this book.

08850 is registered for use between Battersby and Whitby only, for rescue purposes.

Non-standard liveries/numbering:

08308 All over ScotRail "Caledonian Sleeper" purple.
08442 Dark grey lower bodyside with light grey upper bodyside. Carries no number.
08480 Yellow with a red bodyside band. Carries number "TOTON No 1".
08616 Carries number 3783.
08701 Carries number "Tyne 100".
08721 As **B**, but with a black roof & "Express parcels" branding with red & yellow stripe.
08824 Carries number "IEMD01".
08836 Carries no number.

Originally numbered in series D3000–D4192.

Class 08/0. Standard Design.

08077	**FL**	P	DHLT	LH
08308 a	**0**	RL	MRSO	IS
08389 a	**E**	DB	WNTS	TO
08393 a	**E**	DB	WNYX	TO
08401 a	**DG**	DB	WNXX	IM

08405 a†	E	DB	WSSI	TO	
08410 a	GL	FG	EFSH	PZ	
08428 a	E	DB	WSSN	TO	
08442 a	O	DB	WSXX	EH	RICHARD J. WENHAM EASTLEIGH DEPOT
					DECEMBER 1989–JULY 1999
08451	GB	AM	ATZZ	MA	
08454	K	AM	ATLO	WB	
08466 a†	E	DB	WNXX	TO	
08472 a	WA	WA	RFSH	EC	
08480 a	O	DB	WSSK	TO	
08482 a	E	DB	WNXX	TO	
08483 a	GL	FG	EFSH	OO	DUSTY Driver David Miller
08495 †	E	DB	WSSN	TO	NOEL KIRTON OBE
08500	E	DR	WNTS	DR	
08512 a	E	DB	WNXX	DR	
08514 a	E	DB	WNTS	DR	
08516 a	E	DB	WSXX	BK	
08525	MA	EM	EMSL	NL	
08530	FL	P	DFLS	FD	
08531 a	DG	P	DFLS	FD	
08538	DG	X	WNXX	BS	
08561	B	DB	WNXX	TO	
08567	E	DB	WSSI	TO	
08569	E	DB	WNXX	DR	
08571 a	WA	WA	HBSH	BN	
08575	FL	P	DHLT	SZ	
08577	E	X	WNXX	BS	
08578	E	DB	WSSI	TO	
08580	E	DB	WNXX	BS	
08585	FL	P	DFLS	FD	Vicky
08593	E	DB	WNTS	TO	
08596 a†	WA	WA	RFSH	BN	
08597	E	DB	WNXX	TE	
08605	E	DB	WSSI	TO	
08611	V	AM	ATLO	LL	DOWNHILL C.S.
08615	WA	WA	RFSH	EC	
08616	LM	LM	EJLO	TS	TYSELEY 100
08617	K	AM	ATLO	WB	
08623	E	DB	WSSN	TO	
08624	FL	P	DFLS	FD	
08630	E	DB	WNYX	TO	BOB BROWN
08632	E	DB	WNYX	TO	
08633	E	DB	WSSN	TO	
08641	FB	FG	EFSH	LA	
08644	GL	FG	EFSH	LA	
08645	FB	FG	EFSH	LA	Mike Baggott
08646	F	DB	WNTS	MG	
08651 a	DG	X	WNXX	BS	
08653	E	DB	WNYX	TO	
08662	E	DB	WNTS	SP	
08663 a	GL	FG	EFSH	PM	

08664		E	DB	WNTS	DR	
08669	a	**WA**	WA	RFSH	ZB	Bob Machin
08676		E	DB	WSSN	TO	
08685		E	DB	WNTS	IM	
08690		**MA**	EM	EMSL	NL	
08691		**FL**	FL	DFLS	FD	Terri
08696	a	**G**	AM	ATLO	MA	LONGSIGHT TMD
08698	a	E	DB	WNXX	TE	
08701	a	**RX**	DB	WNYX	TO	
08703	a	E	DB	WSSI	TO	
08706	†	E	DB	WSSI	TO	
08709		E	DB	WNTS	BS	
08711	k	**RX**	DB	WSSN	TO	
08714		E	DB	WSSI	TO	Cambridge
08721		**0**	AM	ATLO	MA	M.A. Smith
08724		**WA**	WA	HBSH	NL	
08735	†	E	DB	WSSN	TO	
08737	a	E	DB	WNYX	MG	
08742	†	**RX**	DB	WNYX	TO	
08745		**FE**	P	DHLT	SZ (S)	
08752	†	E	DB	WNYX	TO	
08757		**RG**	DB	WSSN	TO	
08765		E	DB	WNXX	EH	
08770	a	**DG**	DB	WNXX	MG	
08776	a	**DG**	DB	WNXX	TE	
08782	a†	**CU**	DB	WSSN	TO	CASTLETON WORKS
08783		E	DB	WNTR	TO	
08784	†	E	DB	WSSN	TO	
08785	a	**FL**	P	DFLS	FD	
08786	a	**DG**	DB	WNXX	DR	
08788		**RT**	RL	MRSO	IS	
08790		**B**	AM	ATLO	OY	STARLET
08795		**GL**	FG	EFSH	LE	
08798		E	DB	WNTS	TO	
08799	a	E	DB	WNYX	TO	
08802	†	E	DB	WSSN	TO	
08804		E	DB	WNYX	TO	
08805		**B**	LM	EJLO	SO	CONCORDE
08822		**GL**	FG	EFSH	PM	
08824	ak	**K**	DB	WSXX	CE	
08828	a	E	DB	WNXX	BS	
08836		**FB**	FG	EFSH	OO	
08842		E	DB	WNTS	BS	
08844		E	DB	WNTS	BS	CHRIS WREN 1955–2002
08847		**CD**	RL	MRSO	NC	
08850		**B**	NY	MBDL	NY	
08853	a	**WA**	WA	RFSH	ZB	
08854	†	E	DB	WNTS	MG	
08856		**B**	DB	WNXX	DC	
08865		E	DB	WSSK	TO	
08866		E	DB	WNTS	DR	

08874	**SL**	RL	MRSO	NC	
08877	**DG**	DB	WSXX	SP	
08879	**E**	DB	WSSN	TO	
08886 †	**E**	DB	WSSN	TO	
08887 a	**VP**	AM	ATZZ	MA	
08888	**E**	DB	WSSN	TO	
08891	**FL**	P	DHLT	LH	J.R 1951–2005
08897	**E**	DB	WNXX	DR	
08899	**MA**	EM	EMSL	DY	
08904	**E**	DB	WNYX	TO	
08905	**E**	DB	WNTS	BS	
08907	**E**	DB	WSSN	TO	
08908	**MM**	EM	EMSL	NL	
08909	**E**	DB	WNYX	TO	
08918	**DG**	DB	WNTS	TO	
08921 †	**E**	DB	WNYX	TO	
08922	**DG**	DB	WSSN	TO	
08924	**E**	DB	WNXX	TY	
08925	**B**	DB	WNXX	DR	
08934 a	**VP**	AM	ATLO	WB	
08941	**E**	DB	WNXX	DR	
08948 c	**EP**	EU	GPSS	TI	
08950	**MA**	EM	EMSL	NL (S)	
08951 †	**E**	DB	WNTS	TO	
08954	**F**	DB	WNXX	TO	

Class 08/9. Reduced height cab. Converted 1985–1987 by BR at Landore.

08993	**E**	DB	WSSN	TO
08994 a	**E**	DB	WSSI	TO
08995 a	**E**	DB	WSSK	TO

CLASS 09   BR/ENGLISH ELECTRIC   0-6-0

Built: 1959–1962 by BR at Darlington or Horwich Works.
Engine: English Electric 6KT of 298 kW (400 h.p.) at 680 r.p.m.
Main Generator: English Electric 801.
Traction Motors: English Electric 506.
Maximum Tractive Effort: 111 kN (25000 lbf).
Continuous Tractive Effort: 39 kN (8800 lbf) at 11.6 m.p.h.

Power At Rail: 201 kW (269 h.p.).	**Train Brakes:** Air & vacuum.
Brake Force: 19 t.	**Dimensions:** 8.92 x 2.59 m.
Weight: 49 t.	**Wheel Diameter:** 1372 mm.
Design Speed: 27 m.p.h.	**Maximum Speed:** 27 m.p.h.
Fuel Capacity: 3037 litres.	**RA:** 5.
Train Supply: Not equipped.	**Multiple Working:** Not equipped.

Class 09/0 were originally numbered D3665–D3671, D3719–D3721, D4099–D4114.

Class 09/0. Built as Class 09.

09001	**E**	DB	WNTS	DR	
09005 k	**E**	DB	WNTS	TO	
09006	**E**	DB	WNTS	DR	
09007	**ML**	DB	WNTS	WN	
09008	**E**	X	WNXX	BS	
09009	**E**	DB	WNXX	TO	
09011	**DG**	DB	WNTS	MG	
09013	**DG**	DB	WNTS	TO	
09014	**DG**	DB	WNTS	DR	
09015	**E**	DB	WNTS	MG	
09016	**E**	X	WNXX	BZ	
09017	**E**	DB	WNTS	TO	
09019	**ML**	DB	WNYX	TO	
09020	**E**	DB	WNTS	MG	
09022 a	**E**	DB	WSSI	TO	
09023 a	**E**	DB	WNTS	IM	
09024	**ML**	DB	WNTS	EH	
09026 a	**G**	SN	HWSU	BI	Cedric Wares

Class 09/1. Converted from Class 08. 110 V electrical equipment.
Converted: 1992–1993 by RFS Industries, Kilnhurst.

09101	(08833)	**DG**	DB WNTS	DR	
09102	(08832)	**DG**	DB WNTS	MG	
09105	(08835)	**DG**	DB WNTS	DR	
09106	(08759)	**E**	DB WSSI	TO	
09107	(08845)	**E**	DB WNTS	DR	

Class 09/2. Converted from Class 08. 90 V electrical equipment.
Converted: 1992 by RFS Industries, Kilnhurst.

09201	(08421)	ak	**DG**	DB WSSN	TO
09202	(08732)		**DG**	DB WNXX	DR
09203	(08781)		**DG**	DB WNXX	CE
09204	(08717)		**DG**	DB WNXX	TY
09205	(08620)		**DG**	DB WNTS	TE

CLASS 20   ENGLISH ELECTRIC   Bo-Bo

Built: 1957–1968 by English Electric at Vulcan Foundry, Newton-le-Willows or by Robert Stephenson & Hawthorns at Darlington.
Engine: English Electric 8SVT Mk. II of 746 kW (1000 h.p.) at 850 r.p.m.
Main Generator: English Electric 819/3C.
Traction Motors: English Electric 526/5D or 526/8D.
Maximum Tractive Effort: 187 kN (42000 lbf).
Continuous Tractive Effort: 111 kN (25000 lbf) at 11 m.p.h.

Power At Rail: 574 kW (770 h.p.).	**Train Brakes:** Air & vacuum.
Brake Force: 35 t.	**Dimensions:** 14.25 x 2.67 m.
Weight: 73.4–73.5 t.	**Wheel Diameter:** 1092 mm.
Design Speed: 75 m.p.h.	**Maximum Speed:** 75 m.p.h.
Fuel Capacity: 1727 litres.	**RA:** 5.

▲ Wabtec-liveried 08669 "Bob Machin" shunts newly reliveried East Coast Mark 4s in Doncaster West Yard on 24/07/10. **Robert Pritchard**

▼ Unbranded DRS-liveried 20304/302 top-and-tail a train of new Metropolitan S Stock with 20301/305 at Wychnor, south of Burton-on-Trent, on 14/07/10. The train was running as 8X09 Old Dalby–Neasden (LUL). **Stacey Thew**

▲ Network Rail yellow-liveried 31285 passes Acton Central with 4Z03 Derby RTC–Selhurst test train on 09/08/10.　　**Antony Guppy**

▼ West Coast Railway Company maroon-liveried 33207 "Jim Martin" passes Cefn, near Welshpool with 5Z71 08.51 Machynlleth–Crewe ecs after the end of the Cambrian steam season.　　**Richard Jones**

▲ DRS-liveried 37510 and 37667 pass Thurmaston, Leicester, with 6Z90 08.37 Tyne Dock–Sheerness loaded scrap on 21/04/10.

Dave Gommersall

▲ First Great Western HST 43004 and 43137 (nearest camera) is seen on the single-track Weston loop, near Weston-super-Mare station, with the 08.40 Exeter St Davids–London Paddington on 16/08/10.

Robert Pritchard

▲ The Network Rail New Measurement Train, with power cars 43013 and 43062 passes through the New Forest near Beaulieu Road on 22/04/10 working as 1Z23 14.51 Basingstoke–Weymouth–Old Oak Common. **Andrew Mist**

▼ Carrying the colourful yellow & orange Colas Rail livery, 47739 "Robin of Templecombe" passes Lower Moor, near Pershore, with a 4Z47 Chaddesden Yard–Long Marston movement of wagons for storage on 21/04/10. **Dave Gommersall**

▲ West Coast Railway Company maroon-liveried 47786 "Roy Castle OBE" crosses Rannoch Viaduct with the 13.32 Edinburgh–Spean Bridge leg of a Royal Scotsman excursion on 18/06/10.
Neil Gibson

▲ BR Blue-liveried Deltic 55022 "ROYAL SCOTS GREY" passes Cromwell (between Retford and Newark) with the 13.50 Newcastle–London King's Cross Spitfire "The Norseman" charter on 11/09/10.

Lindsay Atkinson

▲ DRS-liveried 57009 passes Hawthorn Dene, south of Seaham on the Durham Coast line, with the 15.55 Sunderland–Darlington loco-hauled shuttle on 08/08/10. This service was run in connection with the Tall Ships event being held in Hartlepool.

Neil Gibson

Train Supply: Not equipped.   **Multiple Working:** Blue Star.

Originally numbered in series D8007–D8190, D8315–D8325.

Non-standard liveries/numbering:

20088 & 20105 RFS grey (20088 carries No. 2017 & 20105 carries Nos. 2016 and 36).
20132 Carries number D8132.
20906 Carries no number.

Class 20/0. Standard Design.

20016	B	HN	HNRS	LM	
20032	B	HN	HNRS	LM	
20057	B	HN	HNRS	LM	
20072	B	HN	HNRS	LM	
20081	B	HN	HNRS	LM	
20088	0	HN	HNRS	LM	
20092	U	HN	HNRS	BH	
20096	B	HN	HNRL	BH	
20107	B	HN	HNRS	BH	
20121	B	HN	HNRS	BH	
20132	G	HN	HNRS	HP	Barrow Hill Depot
20142	B	2L	MOLO	BH	
20189	G	20	MOLO	SK	
20197	B	HN	HNRS	LM	
20227	F0	2L	MOLO	SK	

Class 20/3. Direct Rail Services refurbished locos. Details as Class 20/0 except:

Refurbished: 1995–1996 by Brush Traction at Loughborough (20301–20305) or 1997–1998 by RFS(E) at Doncaster (20306–20315). Disc indicators or headcode panels removed.

Train Brakes: Air.   **Maximum Speed:** 75 m.p.h.
Weight: 76 t.   **Fuel Capacity:** 2900 (+ 4909) litres.
Brake Force: 35 t.   **RA:** 5 (+ 6).
Multiple Working: DRS system.

20301	(20047)	+	**DR**	DR GBEE	KM	Max Joule 1958–1999
20302	(20084)		**DR**	DR GBEE	KM	
20303	(20127)	+	**DR**	DR XHSS	BH	
20304	(20120)		**DR**	DR GBEE	KM	
20305	(20095)		**DR**	DR GBEE	KM	Gresty Bridge
20306	(20131)	+	**DR**	DR XHSS	BH	
20307	(20128)	+	**DR**	DR XHSS	CS	
20308	(20187)	+	**DS**	DR XHNC	KM	
20309	(20075)	+	**DS**	DR XHSS	BH	
20310	(20190)	+	**DR**	DR XHSS	CS	
20311	(20102)	+	**DR**	DR XHSS	CS	
20312	(20042)	+	**DS**	DR XHSS	CS	
20313	(20194)	+	**DR**	DR XHSS	CS	
20314	(20117)	+	**DS**	DR XHSS	CS	
20315	(20104)	+	**DR**	DR XHSS	CR	

Class 20/9. Harry Needle Railroad Company (former Hunslet-Barclay/DRS) locos. Details as Class 20/0 except:

Refurbished: 1989 by Hunslet-Barclay at Kilmarnock.
Train Brakes: Air.   **Fuel Capacity:** 1727 (+ 4727) litres.
RA: 5 (+ 6).

20901	(20101)		F	HN HNRL	BH
20902	(20060)	+	DR	HN HNRS	LM
20903	(20083)	+	DR	HN HNRS	LM
20904	(20041)		DR	HN HNRS	BH
20905	(20225)	+	F	HN HNRL	BH
20906	(20219)		DR	HN HNRS	WH

CLASS 25 BR/BEYER PEACOCK/SULZER Bo-Bo

Built: 1965 by Beyer Peacock at Gorton.
Engine: Sulzer 6LDA28-B of 930 kW (1250 h.p.) at 750 r.p.m.
Main Generator: AEI RTB15656.   **Traction Motors:** AEI 253AY.
Maximum Tractive Effort: 200 kN (45000 lbf).
Continuous Tractive Effort: 93 kN (20800 lbf) at 17.1 m.p.h.
Power At Rail: 708 kW (949 h.p.).   **Train Brakes:** Air & vacuum.
Brake Force: 38 t.   **Dimensions:** 15.39 x 2.73 m.
Weight: 71.5 t.   **Wheel Diameter:** 1143 mm.
Design Speed: 90 m.p.h.   **Maximum Speed:** 60 m.p.h.
Fuel Capacity: 2270 litres.   **RA:** 5.
Train Supply: Not equipped.   **Multiple Working:** Blue Star.

Original number is D7628, which the loco currently carries.

Note: Only certified for use on Network Rail metals between Whitby and Battersby, as an extension of North Yorkshire Moors Railway services.

25278	GG	NY MBDL	NY	SYBILLA

CLASS 31 BRUSH/ENGLISH ELECTRIC A1A-A1A

Built: 1958–1962 by Brush Traction at Loughborough.
Engine: English Electric 12SVT of 1100 kW (1470 h.p.) at 850 r.p.m.
Main Generator: Brush TG160-48.   **Traction Motors:** Brush TM73-68.
Maximum Tractive Effort: 160 kN (35900 lbf).
Continuous Tractive Effort: 83 kN (18700 lbf) at 23.5 m.p.h.
Power At Rail: 872 kW (1170 h.p.).   **Train Brakes:** Air & vacuum.
Brake Force: 49 t.   **Dimensions:** 17.30 x 2.67 m.
Weight: 106.7–111 t.   **Wheel Diameter:** 1092/1003 mm.
Design Speed: 90 m.p.h.   **Maximum Speed:** 90 m.p.h.
Fuel Capacity: 2409 litres.   **RA:** 5 or 6.
Train Supply: Not equipped.   **Multiple Working:** Blue Star.

Originally numbered D5520–D5699, D5800–D5862 (not in order).

Non-standard numbering:

31190 Also carries number D5613.

Class 31/1. Standard Design. RA: 5.

31105	**Y**	NR	QADD	ZA	
31106 a	**B**	HJ	RVLO	ZA	
31128	**B**	NS	NRLO	BH	CHARYBDIS
31190	**G**	BA	HTLX	WH	
31233 a	**Y**	NR	QADD	ZA	
31285	**Y**	NR	QADD	ZA	

Class 31/4. Electric Train Supply equipment. RA: 6.
Train Supply: Electric, index 66.

31422	**IC**	BA	RVLO	ZA (S)	
31452	**BA**	BA	RVLO	ZA	
31454	**IC**	BA	RVLO	ZA	
31459	**K**	RE	RVLO	ZA	CERBERUS
31465	**Y**	NR	QADD	ZA	
31468	**FR**	BA	RVLO	WO (S)	HYDRA

Class 31/6. ETS through wiring and controls. RA: 5.

31601 (31186)	**BA**	BA	RVLO	ZA	
31602 (31191)	**Y**	RE	RVLO	ZA	DRIVER DAVE GREEN

CLASS 33 BRCW/SULZER Bo-Bo

Built: 1960–1962 by the Birmingham Railway Carriage & Wagon Company at Smethwick.
Engine: Sulzer 8LDA28 of 1160 kW (1550 h.p.) at 750 r.p.m.
Main Generator: Crompton Parkinson CG391B1.
Traction Motors: Crompton Parkinson C171C2.
Maximum Tractive Effort: 200 kN (45000 lbf).
Continuous Tractive Effort: 116 kN (26000 lbf) at 17.5 m.p.h.
Power At Rail: 906 kW (1215 h.p.). **Train Brakes:** Air & vacuum.
Brake Force: 35 t. **Dimensions:** 15.47 x 2.82 (2.64 m. 33/2).
Weight: 76-78 t. **Wheel Diameter:** 1092 mm.
Design Speed: 85 m.p.h. **Maximum Speed:** 85 m.p.h.
Fuel Capacity: 3410 litres. **RA:** 6.
Train Supply: Electric, index 48 (750 V DC only).
Multiple Working: Blue Star.

Originally numbered in series D6500–D6597 but not in order.

Class 33/0. Standard Design.

33025	**WC**	WC	MBDL	CS	Glen Falloch
33029	**WC**	WC	MBDL	CS (S)	Glen Loy
33030	**DR**	WC	MBDL	CS (S)	

Class 33/2. Built to former Loading Gauge of Tonbridge–Battle Line.
Equipped with slow speed control.

33207	**WC**	WC	MBDL	CS	Jim Martin

CLASS 37   ENGLISH ELECTRIC   Co-Co

Built: 1960–1966 by English Electric at Vulcan Foundry, Newton-le-Willows or by Robert Stephenson & Hawthorns at Darlington.
Engine: English Electric 12CSVT of 1300 kW (1750 h.p.) at 850 r.p.m.
Main Generator: English Electric 822/10G.
Traction Motors: English Electric 538/A.
Maximum Tractive Effort: 245 kN (55500 lbf).
Continuous Tractive Effort: 156 kN (35000 lbf) at 13.6 m.p.h.
Power At Rail: 932 kW (1250 h.p.)   **Train Brakes:** Air & vacuum.
Brake Force: 50 t.   **Dimensions:** 18.75 x 2.74 m.
Weight: 102.8–108.4 t.   **Wheel Diameter:** 1092 mm.
Design Speed: 90 m.p.h.   **Maximum Speed:** 80 m.p.h.
Fuel Capacity: 4046 (+ 7678) litres.   **RA:** 5 (§ 6).
Train Supply: Not equipped.
Multiple Working: Blue Star († DRS system).

Originally numbered D6600–D6608, D6700–D6999 (not in order).

Note: Class 37s in use abroad are listed in section 6 of this book).

Non-standard liveries/numbering:

37402 Light grey lower bodyside & dark grey upper bodyside.
37411 Also carries number D6990.

Class 37/0. Standard Design. Details as above.

37038 †	**DR**	DR	XHNC	KM	
37042 +	**E**	DB	WNXX	DR	
37057 +	**E**	HN	HNRS	BH	
37059 a+†	**DS**	DR	XHNC	KM	
37069 a+†	**DS**	DR	XHNC	KM	
37087 a†	**DR**	DR	XHNC	KM	Keighley & Worth Valley Railway 40th Anniversary 1968–2008
37165 a+	**CE**	WC	MBDL	CS (S)	
37194 †	**DS**	DR	XHNC	KM	
37197	**DS**	DR	XHHP	BH	
37198 +	**Y**	NR	MBDL	GCR	
37214	**WC**	WC	MBDL	CS (S)	Loch Laidon
37218 †	**DS**	DR	XHNC	KM	
37229 †	**DS**	DR	XHNC	KM	Jonty Jarvis 8-12-1998 to 18-3-2005
37259 †	**DS**	DR	XHNC	KM	
37261 a+†	**DR**	DR	XHSS	CS	

Class 37/4. Refurbished with electric train supply equipment. Main generator replaced by alternator. Regeared (CP7) bogies. Details as Class 37/0 except:
Main Alternator: Brush BA1005A.   **Power At Rail:** 935 kW (1254 h.p.).
Traction Motors: English Electric 538/5A.
Maximum Tractive Effort: 256 kN (57440 lbf).
Continuous Tractive Effort: 184 kN (41250 lbf) at 11.4 m.p.h.
Weight: 107 t.   **Design Speed:** 80 m.p.h.
Fuel Capacity: 7678 litres.
Train Supply: Electric, index 30.

37401 r	E	DB	WFMU	CE	
37402	0	DB	WNXX	TO	Bont Y Bermo
37405 r	E	DB	WNTS	TO	
37406 r	E	DB	WNXX	CD	The Saltire Society
37409 a	DS	DR	XHNC	KM	Lord Hinton
37410 r	E	DB	WNTS	ZJ	
37411	G	DB	WNTS	EH	CAERPHILLY CASTLE/CASTELL CAERFFILI
37412	F	DR	XHSS	LM	
37415	E	HN	HNRS	LM	
37416	GS	DB	WNXX	EH	
37417 ra	E	DB	WNXX	EH	
37419	DB	DB	WFMU	TO	
37422 r	E	DB	WNTS	TO	Cardiff Canton
37423 †	DS	DR	XHNC	KM	Spirit of the Lakes
37425	BL	DB	WFMU	TO	Pride of the Valleys/ Balchder y Cymoedd
37426	E	DB	WNXX	CD	
37427 r	E	DB	WNXX	TY	
37428	GS	HN	HNRS	LM	

Class 37/5. Refurbished without train supply equipment. Main generator replaced by alternator. Regeared (CP7) bogies. Details as Class 37/4 except:
Maximum Tractive Effort: 248 kN (55590 lbf).
Weight: 106.1–110.0 t.

37503 r§	E	DB	WNXX	DR	
37510 a†	DS	DR	XHNC	KM	
37516 s	WC	WC	MBDL	CS	
37517 as	LH	WC	MBDL	CS (S)	
37521 r§	E	DB	WNXX	DR	

Class 37/6. Originally refurbished for Nightstar services. Main generator replaced by alternator. UIC jumpers. Details as Class 37/5 except:
Maximum Speed: 90 m.p.h.   **Train Brake:** Air.
Train Supply: Not equipped, but electric through wired.
Multiple Working: DRS system.

37601	DS	DR	XHNC	KM	Class 37-'Fifty'
37602	DS	DR	XHSS	BH	
37603	DS	DR	XHNC	KM	
37604	DS	DR	XHNC	KM	
37605	DR	DR	XHSS	CS	
37606	DR	DR	XHSS	CR	
37607	DR	DR	XHNC	KM	
37608	DS	DR	XHNC	KM	
37609	DR	DR	XHNC	KM	
37610	DS	DR	XHNC	KM	T.S.(Ted) Cassady 14.5.61–6.4.08
37611	DS	DR	XHNC	KM	
37612	DR	DR	XHSS	CS	

Class 37/5 continued.

| 37667 s† | DS | DR | XHNC | KM | |
| 37668 s | E | WC | MBDL | CS (S) | |

37669	r	**E**	DB	WNXX	TO	
37670	r	**DB**	DB	WNXX	CD	St. Blazey T&RS Depot
37671	a	**F**	DB	WNXX	TY	
37676	a	**WC**	WC	MBDL	CS	Loch Rannoch
37680	a§	**F**	HN	HNRS	HP	
37682	rt†	**DS**	DR	XHNC	KM	
37683	a	**DS**	DR	XHHP	CQ	
37685	a	**WC**	WC	MBDL	CS	
37688	†	**DS**	DR	XHNC	KM	Kingmoor TMD
37689	a§	**F**	X	WNXX	DR	
37693	as	**F**	DB	WNXX	TY	
37696	as	**F**	HN	HNRS	LM	

Class 37/7. Refurbished locos. Main generator replaced by alternator. Regeared (CP7) bogies. Ballast weights added. Details as Class 37/5 except:
Main Alternator: GEC G564AZ (37796–803) Brush BA1005A (others).
Weight: 120 t. **RA:** 7.

37706		**WC**	WC	MBDL	CS	
37707		**E**	DB	WNXX	BS	
37709		**F**	X	WNXX	MH	
37710		**LH**	WC	MBDL	CS (S)	
37712	a	**WC**	WC	MBDL	CS (S)	
37886		**E**	X	WNXX	MH	Sir Dyfed/County of Dyfed
37891	a	**F**	DB	WNXX	TY	
37895	s	**E**	DB	WNXX	BS	
37898	s	**F**	HN	HNRS	LM	

Class 97/3. Class 37s refurbished for Network Rail for use on the Cambrian Lines pilot ERTMS signalling project. Details as Class 37/0.

97301	(37100)	e	**Y**	NR	QETS	ZA	
97302	(37170)	e	**Y**	NR	QETS	ZA	
97303	(37178)	e	**Y**	NR	QETS	ZA	
97304	(37217)	e	**Y**	NR	QETS	ZA	John Tiley

CLASS 40   ENGLISH ELECTRIC   1Co-Co1

Built: 1958–1962 by English Electric at Vulcan Foundry, Newton-le-Willows.
Engine: English Electric 16SVT Mk2 of 1490 kW (2000 h.p.) at 850 r.p.m.
Main Generator: English Electric 822/4C.
Traction Motors: English Electric 526/5D or EE526/7D.
Maximum Tractive Effort: 231 kN (52000 lbf).
Continuous Tractive Effort: 137 kN (30900 lbf) at 18.8 m.p.h.
Power At Rail: 1160 kW (1550 h.p.). | **Train Brakes:** Air & vacuum.
Brake Force: 51 t. | **Dimensions:** 21.18 x 2.78 m.
Weight: 132 t. | **Wheel Diameter:** 914/1143 mm.
Design Speed: 90 m.p.h. | **Maximum Speed:** 90 m.p.h.
Fuel Capacity: 3250 litres. | **RA:** 6.
Train Supply: Steam. | **Multiple Working:** Blue Star.

Originally numbered D345.

| 40145 | **BL** | 40 | ELRD | BQ | East Lancashire Railway |

CLASS 43   BREL/PAXMAN   Bo-Bo

Built: 1975–1982 by BREL at Crewe Works.
Engine: Paxman Valenta 12RP200L of 1680 kW (2250 h.p.) at 1500 r.p.m.
(* Paxman 12VP185 of 1565 kW (2100 h.p.) at 1500 r.p.m.).
(m MTU 16V4000 R41R of 1680kW (2250 h.p.) at 1500 r.p.m.). Fitted to all FGW,
East Coast, CrossCountry and Network Rail power cars.
Main Alternator: Brush BA1001B.
Traction Motors: Brush TMH68–46 or GEC G417AZ, frame mounted.
Maximum Tractive Effort: 80 kN (17980 lbf).
Continuous Tractive Effort: 46 kN (10340 lbf) at 64.5 m.p.h.
Power At Rail: 1320 kW (1770 h.p.).   **Train Brakes:** Air.
Brake Force: 35 t.   **Dimensions:** 17.79 x 2.74 m.
Weight: 70.25 t.   **Wheel Diameter:** 1020 mm.
Design Speed: 125 m.p.h.   **Maximum Speed:** 125 m.p.h.
Fuel Capacity: 4500 litres.   **RA:** 5.
Train Supply: Three-phase electric.
Multiple Working: Within class, jumpers at non-driving end only.

Notes: † Buffer fitted.

43013, 43014 & 43062 are fitted with measuring apparatus & front-end cameras.

43002	m **FB**	A	EFPC	LA	
43003	m **FB**	A	EFPC	LA	ISAMBARD KINGDOM BRUNEL
43004	m **FB**	A	EFPC	LA	First for the future/
					First ar gyfer y dyfodol
43005	m **FB**	A	EFPC	LA	
43009	m **FB**	A	EFPC	LA	First transforming travel
43010	m **FB**	A	EFPC	LA	
43012	m **FB**	A	EFPC	LA	
43013	m† **Y**	P	QCAR	EC	
43014	m† **Y**	P	QCAR	EC	
43015	m **FB**	A	EFPC	LA	
43016	m **FB**	A	EFPC	LA	
43017	m **FB**	A	EFPC	LA	
43018	m **FB**	A	EFPC	LA	
43020	m **FB**	A	EFPC	LA	
43021	m **FB**	A	EFPC	LA	David Austin – Cartoonist
43022	m **FB**	A	EFPC	LA	
43023	m **FB**	A	EFPC	LA	
43024	m **FB**	A	EFPC	LA	
43025	m **FB**	A	EFPC	LA	IRO The Institution of Railway
					Operators 2000–2010 TEN YEARS
					PROMOTING OPERATIONAL EXCELLENCE
43026	m **FB**	A	EFPC	LA	
43027	m **FB**	A	EFPC	LA	Glorious Devon
43028	m **FB**	A	EFPC	LA	
43029	m **FB**	A	EFPC	LA	
43030	m **FB**	A	EFPC	LA	Christian Lewis Trust
43031	m **FB**	A	EFPC	LA	
43032	m **FB**	A	EFPC	LA	

43033	m	**FB**	A	EFPC	LA	Driver Brian Cooper
						15 June 1947–5 October 1999
43034	m	**FB**	A	EFPC	LA	TravelWatch SouthWest
43035	m	**FB**	A	EFPC	LA	
43036	m	**FB**	A	EFPC	LA	
43037	m	**FB**	A	EFPC	LA	PENYDARREN
43040	m	**FB**	A	EFPC	LA	Bristol St. Philip's Marsh
43041	m	**FB**	A	EFPC	OO	
43042	m	**FB**	A	EFPC	OO	
43043	*	**MN**	P	EMPC	NL	
43044	*	**ST**	P	EMPC	NL	
43045	*	**MN**	P	EMPC	NL	
43046	*	**ST**	P	EMPC	NL	
43047	*	**MN**	P	EMPC	NL	
43048	*	**ST**	P	EMPC	NL	T.C.B. Miller MBE
43049	*	**ST**	P	EMPC	NL	Neville Hill
43050	*	**ST**	P	EMPC	NL	
43052	*	**ST**	P	EMPC	NL	
43053	m	**FB**	P	EFPC	LE	University of Worcester
43054	*	**ST**	P	EMPC	NL	
43055	*	**ST**	P	EMPC	NL	
43056	m	**FB**	P	EFPC	LE	The Royal British Legion
43058	*	**ST**	P	EMPC	NL	
43059	*	**MN**	P	EMPC	NL	
43060	*	**MN**	P	EMPC	NL	
43061	*	**ST**	P	EMPC	NL	
43062	m	**Y**	P	QCAR	EC	John Armitt
43063	m	**FB**	P	EFPC	OO	
43064	*	**ST**	P	EMPC	NL	
43066	*	**ST**	P	EMPC	NL	
43069	m	**FB**	P	EFPC	OO	
43070	m	**FB**	P	EFPC	OO	The Corps of Royal Electrical and
						Mechanical Engineers
43071	m	**FB**	P	EFPC	OO	
43072	*	**ST**	P	EMPC	NL	
43073	*	**MN**	P	EMPC	NL	
43074	*	**MN**	P	EMPC	NL	
43075	*	**MN**	P	EMPC	NL	
43076	*	**ST**	P	EMPC	NL	IN SUPPORT OF HELP for HEROES
43078	m	**FB**	P	EFPC	OO	
43079	m	**FB**	P	EFPC	OO	
43081	*	**MN**	P	EMPC	NL	
43082	*	**ST**	P	EMPC	NL	RAILWAY children – THE VOICE FOR
						STREET CHILDREN WORLDWIDE
43083	*	**ST**	P	EMPC	NL	
43084	†	**GC**	A	GCHP	HT	
43086	m	**FB**	P	EFPC	OO	
43087	m	**FB**	P	EFPC	OO	
43088	m	**FB**	P	EFPC	OO	
43089	*	**ST**	P	EMPC	NL	
43091	m	**FB**	P	EFPC	OO	

43092	m	**FB**	FG	EFPC	OO	
43093	m	**FB**	FG	EFPC	OO	
43094	m	**FB**	FG	EFPC	OO	
43097	m	**FB**	FG	EFPC	OO	Environment Agency
43098	m	**FB**	FG	EFPC	OO	
43122	m	**FB**	FG	EFPC	OO	
43123	†	**GC**	A	GCHP	HT	
43124	m	**FB**	A	EFPC	LE	
43125	m	**FB**	A	EFPC	LE	
43126	m	**FB**	A	EFPC	LE	
43127	m	**FB**	A	EFPC	LE	Sir Peter Parker 1924–2002 Cotswold Line 150
43128	m	**FB**	A	EFPC	LE	
43129	m	**FB**	A	EFPC	LE	
43130	m	**FB**	A	EFPC	LE	
43131	m	**FB**	A	EFPC	LE	
43132	m	**FB**	A	EFPC	LE	We Save the Children – Will You?
43133	m	**FB**	A	EFPC	LE	
43134	m	**FB**	A	EFPC	LE	
43135	m	**FB**	A	EFPC	LE	
43136	m	**FB**	A	EFPC	LE	
43137	m	**FB**	A	EFPC	LE	
43138	m	**FB**	A	EFPC	LE	
43139	m	**FB**	A	EFPC	LE	Driver Stan Martin 25 June 1950 – 6 November 2004
43140	m	**FB**	A	EFPC	LE	
43141	m	**FB**	A	EFPC	LE	
43142	m	**FB**	A	EFPC	LE	
43143	m	**FB**	A	EFPC	LE	Stroud 700
43144	m	**FB**	A	EFPC	LE	
43145	m	**FB**	A	EFPC	LE	
43146	m	**FB**	A	EFPC	LE	
43147	m	**FB**	A	EFPC	LE	
43148	m	**FB**	A	EFPC	LE	
43149	m	**FB**	A	EFPC	LE	
43150	m	**FB**	A	EFPC	LE	
43151	m	**FB**	A	EFPC	LE	
43152	m	**FB**	A	EFPC	LE	
43153	m	**FB**	FG	EFPC	OO	
43154	m	**FB**	FG	EFPC	OO	
43155	m	**FB**	FG	EFPC	OO	
43156	m	**FB**	P	EFPC	OO	Dartington International Summer School
43158	m	**FB**	FG	EFPC	OO	
43159	m	**FB**	P	EFPC	OO	
43160	m	**FB**	P	EFPC	OO	
43161	m	**FB**	P	EFPC	OO	
43162	m	**FB**	P	EFPC	OO	
43163	m	**FB**	A	EFPC	OO	Exeter Panel Signal Box 21st Anniversary 2009
43164	m	**FB**	A	EFPC	OO	
43165	m	**FB**	A	EFPC	OO	Prince Michael of Kent

43168	m	**FB**	A	EFPC	OO
43169	m	**FB**	A	EFPC	OO	THE NATIONAL TRUST
43170	m	**FB**	A	EFPC	OO
43171	m	**FB**	A	EFPC	OO
43172	m	**FB**	A	EFPC	OO
43174	m	**FB**	A	EFPC	OO
43175	m	**FB**	A	EFPC	OO	GWR 175th ANNIVERSARY
43176	m	**FB**	A	EFPC	OO
43177	m	**FB**	A	EFPC	OO
43179	m	**FB**	A	EFPC	OO	Pride of Laira
43180	m	**FB**	P	EFPC	OO
43181	m	**FB**	A	EFPC	OO
43182	m	**FB**	A	EFPC	OO
43183	m	**FB**	A	EFPC	OO
43185	m	**FB**	A	EFPC	OO	Great Western
43186	m	**FB**	A	EFPC	OO
43187	m	**FB**	A	EFPC	OO
43188	m	**FB**	A	EFPC	OO
43189	m	**FB**	A	EFPC	OO	RAILWAY HERITAGE TRUST
43190	m	**FB**	A	EFPC	OO
43191	m	**FB**	A	EFPC	OO
43192	m	**FB**	A	EFPC	OO
43193	m	**FB**	P	EFPC	OO
43194	m	**FB**	FG	EFPC	OO
43195	m	**FB**	P	EFPC	OO
43196	m	**FB**	P	EFPC	OO
43197	m	**FB**	P	EFPC	OO
43198	m	**FB**	FG	EFPC	OO	Oxfordshire 2007

Class 43/2. Rebuilt East Coast, CrossCountry and Grand Central power cars.
Power cars have been renumbered by adding 200 to their original number or
400 to their original number (Grand Central).

43206	(43006)	m	**NX**	A	IECP	EC
43207	(43007)	m	**XC**	A	EHPC	EC
43208	(43008)	m	**NX**	A	IECP	EC
43238	(43038)	m	**NX**	A	IECP	EC
43239	(43039)	m	**NX**	A	IECP	EC
43251	(43051)	m	**NX**	P	IECP	EC
43257	(43057)	m	**NX**	P	IECP	EC
43277	(43077)	m	**NX**	P	IECP	EC
43285	(43085)	m	**XC**	P	EHPC	EC
43290	(43090)	m	**NX**	P	IECP	EC	mtu fascination of power
43295	(43095)	m	**NX**	A	IECP	EC
43296	(43096)	m	**NX**	A	IECP	EC
43299	(43099)	m	**NX**	P	IECP	EC
43300	(43100)	m	**NX**	P	IECP	EC	Craigentinny
43301	(43101)	m	**XC**	P	EHPC	EC
43302	(43102)	m	**NX**	P	IECP	EC
43303	(43103)	m	**XC**	P	EHPC	EC
43304	(43104)	m	**XC**	A	EHPC	EC
43305	(43105)	m	**NX**	A	IECP	EC

43306	(43106)	m	**NX**	A	IECP	EC
43307	(43107)	m	**NX**	A	IECP	EC
43308	(43108)	m	**NX**	A	IECP	EC
43309	(43109)	m	**NX**	A	IECP	EC
43310	(43110)	m	**NX**	A	IECP	EC
43311	(43111)	m	**NX**	A	IECP	EC
43312	(43112)	m	**NX**	A	IECP	EC
43313	(43113)	m	**NX**	A	IECP	EC
43314	(43114)	m	**NX**	A	IECP	EC
43315	(43115)	m	**NX**	A	IECP	EC
43316	(43116)	m	**NX**	A	IECP	EC
43317	(43117)	m	**NX**	A	IECP	EC
43318	(43118)	m	**NX**	A	IECP	EC
43319	(43119)	m	**NX**	A	IECP	EC
43320	(43120)	m	**NX**	A	IECP	EC
43321	(43121)	m	**XC**	P	EHPC	EC
43357	(43157)	m	**XC**	P	EHPC	EC
43366	(43166)	m	**XC**	A	EHPC	EC
43367	(43167)	m	**NX**	A	IECP	EC	DELTIC 50 1955–2005
43378	(43178)	m	**XC**	A	EHPC	EC
43384	(43184)	m	**XC**	A	EHPC	EC
43465	(43065)	†m	**GC**	A	GCHP	HT
43467	(43067)	†m	**GC**	A	GCHP	HT
43468	(43068)	†m	**GC**	A	GCHP	HT
43480	(43080)	†m	**GC**	A	GCHP	HT
43484	(43084)	†m	**GC**			
43523	(43123)	†m	**GC**			

CLASS 47   BR/BRUSH/SULZER   Co-Co

Built: 1963–1967 by Brush Traction, at Loughborough or by BR at Crewe Works.
Engine: Sulzer 12LDA28C of 1920 kW (2580 h.p.) at 750 r.p.m.
Main Generator: Brush TG160-60 Mk4 or TM172-50 Mk1.
Traction Motors: Brush TM64-68 Mk1 or Mk1A.
Maximum Tractive Effort: 267 kN (60000 lbf).
Continuous Tractive Effort: 133 kN (30000 lbf) at 26 m.p.h.
Power At Rail: 1550 kW (2080 h.p.).   **Train Brakes:** Air.
Brake Force: 61 t.   **Dimensions:** 19.38 x 2.79 m.
Weight: 111.5–120.6 t.   **Wheel Diameter:** 1143 mm.
Design Speed: 95 m.p.h.
Maximum Speed: 95 m.p.h. (* 75 m.p.h.).
Fuel Capacity: 3273 (+ 5550).   **RA:** 6 or 7.
Train Supply: Not equipped.
Multiple Working: † DRS system, m Green Circle (operational locos only).

Originally numbered in series D1100–D1111, D1500–D1999 but not in order.

Non-standard liveries/numbering:

47270 Also carries number D1971.
47773 Also carries number D1755.
47812 Also carries number D1916.

47815 Also carries number D1748.
47829 "Police" livery of white with a broad red band outlined in yellow.
47851 Also carries number D1648.
47853 "XP64 blue" with red cabside panels. Also carries number D1733.
47972 BR Central Services red & grey.

Class 47/0 (Dual-braked locos) or Class 47/2 (Air-braked locos). Standard Design. Details as above.

47194		**F**	WC	MBDL	CS (S)	
47236 +		**FE**	WC	MBDL	CS (S)	
47237 +		**AZ**	HN	HNRS	GL	
47245 x+m	**WC**	WC	MBDL	CS	
47270		**B**	PO	MBDL	CS	SWIFT
47295 a		**FF**	HN	HNRS	LM	

Class 47/3 (Dual-braked locos) or Class 47/2 (Air-braked locos).
Details as Class 47/0 except: **Weight:** 113.7 t.

47355 m	**K**	WC	MBDL	CS (S)
47368 x	**F**	WC	MBDL	CS (S)
47375 +	**B**	NS	NRLO	BH

Class 47/4. Electric Train Supply equipment.
Details as Class 47/0 except:

Weight: 120.4–125.1 t. **Fuel Capacity:** 3273 (+ 5887) litres.
Train Supply: Electric. ETH 66.   **RA:** 7.

47492 x	**RX**	WC	MBDL	CS (S)	
47500	**WC**	WC	MBDL	CS	
47501 x†+	**DS**	DR	XHAC	KM	Craftsman
47526 x	**BL**	WC	MBDL	CS (S)	
47580 x	**BL**	47	MBDL	TM	County of Essex

Class 47/7. Previously fitted with an older form of TDM.

Details as Class 47/4 except:
Weight: 118.7 t.   **Fuel Capacity:** 5887 litres.
Maximum Speed: 100 m.p.h.

47709 x†	**DS**	DR	XHHP	ZG	
47712 x†	**DS**	DR	XHAC	KM	Pride of Carlisle
47714 xm	**AR**	HN	HNRL	OD	

Class 47/7. Former Railnet dedicated locos. All have twin fuel tanks.

47727 m	**CS**	CS	COLO	WH	Rebecca
47739 m	**CS**	CS	COLO	WH	Robin of Templecombe
47747	**E**	RV	RTLO	CD (S)	
47749 m	**CS**	CS	COLO	WH	Demelza
47760	**WC**	WC	MBDL	CS	
47769	**V**	RV	RTLO	CP	Resolve
47772 x	**RX**	WC	MBDL	CS (S)	
47773 x	**GG**	70	MBDL	TM	
47776 x	**RX**	WC	MBDL	CS (S)	
47786	**WC**	WC	MBDL	CS	Roy Castle OBE

47787	**WC**	WC	MBDL	CS	Windsor Castle
47790 †	**DS**	DR	XHAC	KM	Galloway Princess
47791	**DS**	DR	XHHP	BH	

Class 47/4 continued. RA6. Most fitted with extended-range fuel tanks (+).

47798	**RP**	NM	MBDL	YK	Prince William
47799	**RP**	DB	WNXX	EH	
47802 +†	**DS**	DR	XHAC	KM	Pride of Cumbria
47804	**WC**	WC	MBDL	CS	
47805 +m	**RV**	RV	RTLO	CP	TALISMAN
47810 +	**DS**	DR	XHHP	BH	
47811 +	**GL**	FL	DFLH	BA (S)	
47812 +m	**GG**	RV	RTLO	CP	
47813 +m	**CD**	DR	XHSS	BH	
47815 +m	**GG**	RV	RTLO	CP	GREAT WESTERN
47816 +	**GL**	FL	DFLH	BA (S)	
47818 +	**DS**	DR	XHSS	BH	
47826 +	**WC**	WC	MBDL	CS	
47828 +m	**CD**	DR	XHSS	BH	Joe Strummer
47829 +	**O**	HN	HNRS	LM	
47830 +	**GL**	FL	DFLH	BA (S)	
47832 +†	**DS**	DR	XHAC	KM	Solway Princess
47839 +m	**RV**	RV	RTLO	CP	PEGASUS
47841 +	**DS**	DR	XHHP	BH	
47843 +m	**RV**	RV	RTLO	CP	VULCAN
47847 +m	**BL**	RV	RTLO	EH (S)	
47848 +m	**RV**	RV	RTLO	CP	TITAN STAR
47851 +	**GG**	WC	MBDL	CS	Traction Magazine
47853 +m	**O**	RV	RTLO	CP	RAIL EXPRESS
47854 +	**WC**	WC	MBDL	CS	

CLASS 50   ENGLISH ELECTRIC   Co-Co

Built: 1967–1968 by English Electric at Vulcan Foundry, Newton-le-Willows.
Engine: English Electric 16CVST of 2010 kW (2700 h.p.) at 850 r.p.m.
Main Generator: English Electric 840/4B.
Traction Motors: English Electric 538/5A.
Maximum Tractive Effort: 216 kN (48500 lbf).
Continuous Tractive Effort: 147 kN (33000 lbf) at 23.5 m.p.h.

Power At Rail: 1540 kW (2070 h.p.).	**Train Brakes:** Air & vacuum.
Brake Force: 59 t.	**Dimensions:** 20.88 x 2.78 m.
Weight: 116.9 t.	**Wheel Diameter:** 1092 mm.
Design Speed: 105 m.p.h.	**Maximum Speed:** 90 m.p.h.
Fuel Capacity: 4796 litres.	**RA:** 6.
Train Supply: Electric, index 61.	**Multiple Working:** Orange Square.

Originally numbered D444 & D449.

| 50044 | **GG** | 50 | CFOL | KR | EXETER |
| 50049 | **BL** | 50 | CFOL | CF | Defiance |

CLASS 52   BR/MAYBACH   C-C

Built: 1961–1964 by BR at Swindon Works.
Engine: Two Maybach MD655 of 1007 kW (1350 h.p.) at 1500 r.p.m.
Transmission: Hydraulic. Voith L630rV.
Maximum Tractive Effort: 297 kN (66700 lbf).
Continuous Tractive Effort: 201 kN (45200 lbf) at 14.5 m.p.h.
Power At Rail: 1490 kW (2000 h.p.).   **Train Brakes:** Air & vacuum.
Brake Force: 83 t.   **Dimensions:** 20.7 m x 2.78 m.
Weight: 110 t.   **Wheel Diameter:** 1092 mm.
Design Speed: 90 m.p.h.   **Maximum Speed:** 90 m.p.h.
Fuel Capacity: 3900 litres.   **RA:** 6.
Train Supply: Steam.   **Multiple Working:** Not equipped.

Never allocated a number in the 1972 number series.

Registered on TOPS as No. 89416.

D1015   **M**   DT   MBDL   EH   WESTERN CHAMPION

CLASS 55   ENGLISH ELECTRIC   Co-Co

Built: 1961 by English Electric at Vulcan Foundry, Newton-le-Willows.
Engine: Two Napier-Deltic D18-25 of 1230 kW (1650 h.p.) each at 1500 r.p.m.
Main Generators: Two English Electric 829/1A.
Traction Motors: English Electric 538/A.
Maximum Tractive Effort: 222 kN (50000 lbf).
Continuous Tractive Effort: 136 kN (30500 lbf) at 32.5 m.p.h.
Power At Rail: 1969 kW (2640 h.p.).   **Train Brakes:** Air & vacuum.
Brake Force: 51 t.   **Dimensions:** 21.18 x 2.68 m.
Weight: 100 t.   **Wheel Diameter:** 1092 mm.
Design Speed: 105 m.p.h.   **Maximum Speed:** 100 m.p.h.
Fuel Capacity: 3755 litres.   **RA:** 5.
Train Supply: Electric, index 66.   **Multiple Working:** Not equipped.

Originally numbered D9000.

Registered on TOPS as No. 89500.

55022   **B**   MW   ELRD   BQ   ROYAL SCOTS GREY

CLASS 56   BRUSH/BR/RUSTON   Co-Co

Built: 1976–1984 by Electroputere at Craiova, Romania (as sub contractors for Brush) or BREL at Doncaster or Crewe Works.
Engine: Ruston Paxman 16RK3CT of 2460 kW (3250 h.p.) at 900 r.p.m.
Main Alternator: Brush BA1101A.
Traction Motors: Brush TM73-62.
Maximum Tractive Effort: 275 kN (61800 lbf).
Continuous Tractive Effort: 240 kN (53950 lbf) at 16.8 m.p.h.
Power At Rail: 1790 kW (2400 h.p.).   **Train Brakes:** Air.
Brake Force: 60 t.   **Dimensions:** 19.36 x 2.79 m.
Weight: 126 t.   **Wheel Diameter:** 1143 mm.

Design Speed: 80 m.p.h.
Fuel Capacity: 5228 litres.
Train Supply: Not equipped.

Maximum Speed: 80 m.p.h.
RA: 7.
Multiple Working: Red Diamond.

Note: All equipped with Slow Speed Control.

Non-standard liveries:

56303 All over dark green.
56311 Light grey with yellow cabsides.
56312 Purple with yellow cabsides & green lining.

56006	**B**	DB	WNXX	BH
56007	**FER**	DB	WNXX	CE
56018	**FER**	DB	WNXX	WA
56031	**FER**	DB	WNXX	CD
56032	**FER**	DB	WNXX	CD
56037	**E**	DB	WNXX	CD
56038	**FER**	DB	WNXX	CD
56041	**E**	X	WNXX	DR
56046	**CE**	DB	WNXX	TO
56049	**FER**	DB	WNXX	CD
56051	**FER**	DB	WNXX	CD
56053	**F**	X	WNXX	DR
56054	**F**	DB	WNXX	CD
56055	**LH**	X	WNXX	DR
56058	**FER**	DB	WNXX	CD
56059	**FER**	DB	WNXX	EH
56060	**FER**	DB	WNXX	CD
56065	**FER**	DB	WNXX	CD
56067	**E**	DB	WNXX	CD
56069	**FER**	DB	WNXX	CD
56070	**F**	DB	WNXX	CE
56071	**FER**	DB	WNXX	CD
56072	**F**	X	WNXX	DR
56073	**F**	DB	WNXX	TO
56074	**FER**	DB	WNXX	CD
56077	**LH**	DB	WNXX	CD
56078	**FER**	DB	WNXX	CD
56081	**FER**	DB	WNXX	CD
56083	**LH**	DB	WNXX	CD
56087	**FER**	DB	WNXX	CD
56090	**FER**	DB	WNXX	CD
56091	**FER**	DB	WNXX	EH
56093	**F**	X	WNXX	DR
56094	**FER**	DB	WNXX	CD
56095	**FER**	DB	WNXX	EH
56096	**FER**	DB	WNXX	CD
56099	**F**	X	WNXX	DR
56103	**FER**	DB	WNXX	CD
56104	**FER**	DB	WNXX	CD
56105	**FER**	DB	WNXX	CD
56106	**FER**	DB	WNXX	CD

56107	**LH**	DB	WNXX	CD
56109	**LH**	DB	WNXX	CD
56110	**LH**	X	WNXX	DR
56112	**LH**	DB	WNXX	CE
56113	**FER**	DB	WNXX	CD
56115	**FER**	DB	WNXX	EH
56117	**FER**	DB	WNXX	EH
56119	**E**	X	WNXX	DR
56120	**E**	DB	WNXX	CD
56133	**F**	DB	WNXX	CE

56301	(56045)	**FA**	FA	RCJZ	Hitchin
56302	(56124)	**FA**	FA	RCJZ	Hitchin
56303	(56125)	**0**	RE	RVLO	ZA

56311	(56057)	**0**	BA	HTLX	WF
56312	(56003)	**0**	BA	HTLX	WF	ARTEMIS
56313	(56128)		BA	HTLX	WF (S)
56314	(56114)		BA	HTLX	WH (S)

CLASS 57   BRUSH/GM   Co-Co

Built: 1964–1965 by Brush Traction at Loughborough or BR at Crewe Works as Class 47. Rebuilt 1997–2004 by Brush Traction at Loughborough.
Engine: General Motors 12 645 E3 of 1860 kW (2500 h.p.) at 904 r.p.m.
Main Alternator: Brush BA1101D.
Traction Motors: Brush TM64-68 Mark 1 or Mark 1a.
Maximum Tractive Effort: 244.5 kN (55000 lbf).
Continuous Tractive Effort: 140 kN (31500 lbf) at ?? m.p.h.

Power at Rail: 1507 kW (2025 h.p.).	**Train Brakes:** Air.
Brake Force: 80 t.	**Dimensions:** 19.38 x 2.79 m.
Weight: 120.6 t.	**Wheel Diameter:** 1143 mm.
Design Speed: 75 m.p.h.	**Maximum Speed:** 75 m.p.h.
Fuel Capacity: 5550 litres.	**RA:** 6
Train Supply: Not equipped.	**Multiple Working:** † DRS system.

Class 57/0. No Train Supply Equipment. Rebuilt 1998–2000.

57001	(47356)		**FL**	P	SBXL	BA	
57002	(47322)	†	**DS**	P	XHCK	KM	
57003	(47317)	†	**DS**	P	XHCK	KM	
57004	(47347)	†	**DS**	DR	XHCK	KM	
57005	(47350)		**AZ**	X	HNRL	Cardiff Central (S)	
57006	(47187)		**AZ**	X	HNRL	HT (S)	
57007	(47332)	†	**DS**	P	XHCK	KM	
57008	(47060)	†	**DS**	P	XHCK	KM	Telford International Railfreight Park June 2009
57009	(47079)	†	**DS**	P	XHCK	KM	
57010	(47231)	†	**DS**	P	XHCK	KM	
57011	(47329)	†	**DS**	P	XHCK	KM	
57012	(47204)	†	**DS**	P	XHCK	KM	

Class 57/3. Electric Train Supply Equipment. Virgin Trains locos. Rebuilt 2002–2004. Details as Class 57/0 except:

Engine: General Motors 12645F3B of 2050 kW (2750 h.p.) at 954 r.p.m.
Main Alternator: Brush BA1101F (recovered from a Class 56) or Brush BA1101G.
Fuel Capacity: 5887 litres.   **Train Supply:** Electric, index 100.
Design Speed: 95 m.p.h.   **Maximum Speed:** 95 m.p.h.
Brake Force: 60 t.   **Weight:** 117 t.

Note: 57313–316 are on sub-lease to Arriva Trains Wales and are used on the Holyhead–Cardiff loco-hauled service.

Non-standard livery: 57313 & 57316 All over blue.

57301	(47845)	d	**VT**	P	IWCA	MA	SCOTT TRACY
57302	(47827)	d	**VT**	P	IWCA	MA	VIRGIL TRACY
57303	(47705)	d	**VT**	P	IWCA	MA	ALAN TRACY
57304	(47807)	d	**VT**	P	IWCA	MA	GORDON TRACY
57305	(47822)	d	**VT**	P	IWCA	MA	JOHN TRACY
57306	(47814)	d	**VT**	P	IWCA	MA	JEFF TRACY
57307	(47225)	d	**VT**	P	IWCA	MA	LADY PENELOPE
57308	(47846)	d	**VT**	P	IWCA	MA	TIN TIN
57309	(47806)	d	**VT**	P	IWCA	MA	BRAINS
57310	(47831)	d	**VT**	P	IWCA	MA	KYRANO
57311	(47817)	d	**VT**	P	IWCA	MA	PARKER
57312	(47330)	d	**VT**	P	IWCA	MA	THE HOOD
57313	(47371)	d	**0**	P	IWCA	MA	
57314	(47372)	d	**AB**	P	IWCA	MA	
57315	(47234)	d	**AB**	P	IWCA	MA	
57316	(47290)	d	**0**	P	IWCA	MA	

Class 57/6. Electric Train Supply Equipment. Prototype ETS loco. Rebuilt 2001. Details as Class 57/0 except:

Main Alternator: Brush BA1101E.   **Fuel Capacity:** 3273 litres.
Train Supply: Electric, index 100.   **Weight:** 113 t.
Design Speed: 95 m.p.h.   **Maximum Speed:** 95 m.p.h.
Brake Force: 60 t.

57601	(47825)	**WC**	WC MBDL	CS

Class 57/6. Electric Train Supply Equipment. First Great Western locos. Rebuilt 2004. Details as Class 57/3.

57602	(47337)	**FB**	P	EFOO	OO	Restormel Castle
57603	(47349)	**GL**	P	EFOO	OO	Tintagel Castle
57604	(47209)	**GW**	P	EFOO	OO	PENDENNIS CASTLE
57605	(47206)	**FB**	P	EFOO	OO	Totnes Castle

CLASS 58 BREL/RUSTON Co-Co

Built: 1983–1987 by BREL at Doncaster Works.
Engine: Ruston Paxman 12RK3ACT of 2460 kW (3300 h.p.) at 1000 r.p.m.
Main Alternator: Brush BA1101B. **Traction Motors:** Brush TM73-62.
Maximum Tractive Effort: 275 kN (61800 lbf).
Continuous Tractive Effort: 240 kN (53950 lbf) at 17.4 m.p.h.
Power At Rail: 1780 kW (2387 h.p.). **Train Brakes:** Air.
Brake Force: 60 t. **Dimensions:** 19.13 x 2.72 m.
Weight: 130 t. **Wheel Diameter:** 1120 mm.
Design Speed: 80 m.p.h. **Maximum Speed:** 80 m.p.h.
Fuel Capacity: 4214 litres. **RA:** 7.
Train Supply: Not equipped. **Multiple Working:** Red Diamond.

Notes: All equipped with Slow Speed Control.

Class 58s in use abroad are listed in section 6.

58002	**ML**	DB	WNXX	EH
58008	**ML**	DB	WZTS	EH
58012	**F**	DB	WZTS	TO
58017	**F**	DB	WZTS	EH
58022	**F**	DB	WZTS	CD
58023	**ML**	DB	WZTS	TO
58037	**E**	DB	WZTS	EH
58048	**E**	DB	WZTS	CE

CLASS 59 GENERAL MOTORS Co-Co

Built: 1985 (59001/59002/59004) or 1989 (59005) by General Motors, La Grange, Illinois, USA or 1990 (59101–59104), 1994 (59201) and 1995 (59202–59206) by General Motors, London, Ontario, Canada.
Engine: General Motors 16-645E3C two stroke of 2460 kW (3300 h.p.) at 904 r.p.m.
Main Alternator: General Motors AR11 MLD-D14A.
Traction Motors: General Motors D77B.
Maximum Tractive Effort: 506 kN (113 550 lbf).
Continuous Tractive Effort: 291 kN (65 300 lbf) at 14.3 m.p.h.
Power At Rail: 1889 kW (2533 h.p.). **Train Brakes:** Air.
Brake Force: 69 t. **Dimensions:** 21.35 x 2.65 m.
Weight: 121 t. **Wheel Diameter:** 1067 mm.
Design Speed: 60 (* 75) m.p.h. **Maximum Speed:** 60 (* 75) m.p.h.
Fuel Capacity: 4546 litres. **RA:** 7.
Train Supply: Not equipped. **Multiple Working:** AAR System.

Class 59/0. Owned by Aggregate Industries.

59001	**AI**	AI	XYPO	MD	YEOMAN ENDEAVOUR
59002	**FY**	AI	XYPO	MD	ALAN J DAY
59004	**FY**	AI	XYPO	MD	PAUL A HAMMOND
59005	**AI**	AI	XYPO	MD	KENNETH J PAINTER

Class 59/1. Owned by Hanson Quarry Products.

59101	**HA**	HA	XYPA	MD	Village of Whatley
59102	**HA**	HA	XYPA	MD	Village of Chantry
59103	**HA**	HA	XYPA	MD	Village of Mells
59104	**HA**	HA	XYPA	MD	Village of Great Elm

Class 59/2. Owned by DB Schenker.

59201	*	**E**	DB	WDAK	TO	Vale of York
59202	*	**E**	DB	WDAI	TO	Vale of White Horse
59203	*	**E**	DB	WDAI	TO	Vale of Pickering
59204	*	**E**	DB	WFMU	TO	Vale of Glamorgan
59205	*b	**E**	DB	WDAK	TO	L Keith McNair
59206	*b	**DB**	DB	WDAK	TO	John F. Yeoman Rail Pioneer

CLASS 60   BRUSH/MIRRLEES   Co-Co

Built: 1989–1993 by Brush Traction at Loughborough.
Engine: Mirrlees 8MB275T of 2310 kW (3100 h.p.) at 1000 r.p.m.
Main Alternator: Brush BA1006A.
Traction Motors: Brush TM2161A.
Maximum Tractive Effort: 500 kN (106500 lbf).
Continuous Tractive Effort: 336 kN (71570 lbf) at 17.4 m.p.h.
Power At Rail: 1800 kW (2415 h.p.).   **Train Brakes:** Air.
Brake Force: 74 (+ 62) t.   **Dimensions:** 21.34 x 2.64 m.
Weight: 129 (+ 131) t.   **Wheel Diameter:** 1118 mm.
Design Speed: 62 m.p.h.   **Maximum Speed:** 60 m.p.h.
Fuel Capacity: 4546 (+ 5225) litres.   **RA:** 8.
Train Supply: Not equipped.   **Multiple Working:** Within class.

IMPORTANT NOTE: DB Schenker Fleet Management Unit: As all operational Class 60s are effectively treated as "common user" by DB Schenker, and allocated to operational pools depending on which duties they are on at the time, all operational locos are shown in the WFMU Fleet Management pool here. Details of the other individual pools can be found in the codes section of this book.

Notes: All equipped with Slow Speed Control.

60034, 60063, 60064, 60066, 60072, 60073, 60077, 60079, 60082, 60084, 60090 and 60091 carry their names on one side only.

60500 used to carry the number 60016.

60007, 60044 and 60078 carry EWS logos on their **LH** or **ML** liveries.

Advertising liveries:

60040 Territorial Army Centenary (maroon).
60074 Teenage Cancer Trust (light blue).
60099 Tata Steel (silver).

60001		**E**	DB	WNXX	TO	The Railway Observer
60002	+	**E**	DB	WNTS	CD	High Peak
60003	+	**E**	DB	WNTS	TO	FREIGHT TRANSPORT ASSOCIATION

60004 +	E	DB	WNTR	TO	
60005 +	E	DB	WNTS	TO	
60006	CU	DB	WNXX	TO	
60007	LH	DB	WNTS	CD	
60008	E	DB	WNXX	TO	Sir William McAlpine
60009 +	E	DB	WFMU	TO	
60010 +	E	DB	WFMU	TO	
60011	ML	DB	WFMU	TO	
60012 +	E	DB	WNTS	TO	
60013	EG	DB	WFMU	TO	Robert Boyle
60014	EG	DB	WNXX	TO	
60015 +	EG	DB	WFMU	TO	Bow Fell
60017 +	E	DB	WNTS	TO	Shotton Works Centenary Year 1996
60018	E	DB	WNTS	TO	
60019	E	DB	WFMU	TO	PATHFINDER TOURS 30 YEARS OF RAILTOURING 1973–2003
60020 +	E	DB	WNTS	TO	
60021 +	E	DB	WNTS	TO	
60022 +	E	DB	WNTS	TO	
60023 +	E	DB	WNXX	TO	
60024	E	DB	WNTR	TO	
60025 +	E	DB	WNTS	TO	
60026 +	E	DB	WNTS	TO	
60027 +	E	DB	WNTS	TO	
60028 +	EG	DB	WNTS	CD	John Flamsteed
60029	E	DB	WNTS	CD	Clitheroe Castle
60030 +	E	DB	WNTS	TO	
60031	E	DB	WNXX	TO	
60032	F	DB	WNTS	TO	
60033 +	CU	DB	WNTS	TO	Tees Steel Express
60034	EG	DB	WNTS	TO	Carnedd Llewelyn
60035	E	DB	WNTS	TO	
60036	E	DB	WNTS	TO	GEFCO
60037 +	E	DB	WNTS	TO	
60038 +	E	DB	WNXX	CD	AvestaPolarit
60039	E	DB	WFMU	TO	
60040	AL	DB	WFMU	TO	The Territorial Army Centenary
60041 +	E	DB	WNTS	TO	
60042	E	DB	WNXX	TO	
60043	E	DB	WNTS	CD	
60044	ML	DB	WNTS	TO	
60045	E	DB	WFMS	DR	The Permanent Way Institution
60046 +	EG	DB	WNTS	CD	William Wilberforce
60047	E	DB	WNTS	CD	
60048	E	DB	WFMU	TO	
60049	E	DB	WFMU	TO	
60050	E	DB	WNXX	TO	
60051 +	E	DB	WNTS	TO	
60052 +	E	DB	WNTS	TO	Glofa Twr – The last deep mine in Wales – Tower Colliery
60053	E	DB	WNTS	TO	

60054 +	F	DB	WFMU	TO	Charles Babbage
60055 +	EG	DB	WNXX	CD	Thomas Barnardo
60056 +	EG	DB	WNTS	CD	William Beveridge
60057	EG	DB	WNTS	TO	Adam Smith
60058 +	E	DB	WNXX	TO	
60059 +	LH	DB	WFMU	TO	Swinden Dalesman
60060	EG	DB	WNTS	TO	
60061	F	DB	WNTS	TO	
60062	E	DB	WNTR	TO	
60063	EG	DB	WFMU	TO	James Murray
60064 +	EG	DB	WNTS	TO	Back Tor
60065	E	DB	WNTS	TO	Spirit of JAGUAR
60066	EG	DB	WNTS	TO	John Logie Baird
60067	EG	DB	WNTS	TO	
60068	EG	DB	WNXX	TO	
60069	E	DB	WNTS	TO	Slioch
60070 +	F	DB	WNXX	TO	John Loudon McAdam
60071 +	E	DB	WFMU	TO	Ribblehead Viaduct
60072	EG	DB	WNTS	TO	Cairn Toul
60073	EG	DB	WFMU	TO	Cairn Gorm
60074	AL	DB	WFMU	TO	Teenage Spirit
60075	E	DB	WNXX	TO	
60076	EG	DB	WNTS	CD	
60077 +	EG	DB	WNTS	TO	Canisp
60078	ML	DB	WNXX	TO	
60079	EG	DB	WNTS	CD	Foinaven
60080 +	E	DB	WNXX	TO	
60081 +	GW	DB	WNXX	TO	
60082	EG	DB	WNXX	CD	Mam Tor
60083	E	DB	WNTS	TO	
60084	EG	DB	WFMU	TO	Cross Fell
60085	E	DB	WNTS	TO	MINI Pride of Oxford
60086	EG	DB	WNTS	TO	
60087	E	DB	WNTS	TO	
60088	F	DB	WNTS	TO	
60089 +	E	DB	WNXX	TO	
60090 +	EG	DB	WNTS	TO	Quinag
60091 +	EG	DB	WFMS	TO	An Teallach
60092 +	EG	DB	WNTS	CD	Reginald Munns
60093	E	DB	WNTS	TO	
60094	E	DB	WNTS	TO	Rugby Flyer
60095	EG	DB	WNTS	CD	
60096 +	E	DB	WFMU	TO	
60097 +	E	DB	WNTS	TO	
60098 +	E	DB	WNXX	TO	
60099	AL	DB	WNTR	TO	
60100	E	DB	WNTS	TO	
60500	E	DB	WNTS	TO	

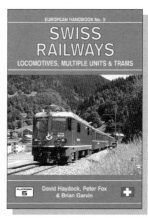

CLASS 66   GENERAL MOTORS/EMD   Co-Co

Built: 1998–2008 by General Motors/EMD, London, Ontario, Canada (Model JT42CWR (low emission locos Model JT42CWRM)).
Engine: General Motors 12N-710G3B-EC two stroke of 2385 kW (3200 h.p.) at 904 r.p.m.
Main Alternator: General Motors AR8/CA6.
Traction Motors: General Motors D43TR.
Maximum Tractive Effort: 409 kN (92000 lbf).
Continuous Tractive Effort: 260 kN (58390 lbf) at 15.9 m.p.h.

Power At Rail: 1850 kW (2480 h.p.).	**Train Brakes:** Air.
Brake Force: 68 t.	**Dimensions:** 21.35 x 2.64 m.
Weight: 127 t.	**Wheel Diameter:** 1120 mm.
Design Speed: 87.5 m.p.h.	**Maximum Speed:** 75 m.p.h.
Fuel Capacity: 6550 litres.	**RA:** 7.
Train Supply: Not equipped.	**Multiple Working:** AAR System.

IMPORTANT NOTE: DB Schenker Fleet Management Unit: As all DB Schenker Class 66s are effectively now treated as "common user" by DB Schenker, and allocated to operational pools depending on which duties they are on at the time, all operational locos are shown in the WFMU Fleet Management pool here. Details of the other individual pools can be found in the codes section of this book.

Notes: All equipped with Slow Speed Control.

Class 66s in use abroad are listed in section 6 of this book. 15 DBS Class 66s (66010/026/028/029/033/042/062/071/072/073/123/191/239/243/249) have returned to the UK for the 2010 Sandite season and are due to return to France.

Advertising livery: 66048 Stobart Rail (two tone blue & white).

Class 66 delivery dates. The Class 66 design has evolved over more than a ten year period with over 400 of these locos in use in the UK. For clarity the delivery dates (by year) for each batch of locos delivered to the UK is as follows:

66001–66250	EWS (now DB Schenker). 1998–2000
66301–66305	Fastline (now stored). 2008
66401–66410	DRS. 2003. Now in use with GB Railfreight or Colas Rail. 66406–410 renumbered 66841–844.
66411–66420	DRS. 2006
66421–66430	DRS. 2007
66431–66434	DRS. 2008
66501–66505	Freightliner. 1999
66506–66520	Freightliner. 2000
66521–66525	Freightliner. 2000 (66521 since scrapped).
66526–66531	Freightliner. 2001
66532–66537	Freightliner. 2001
66538–66543	Freightliner. 2001
66544–66553	Freightliner. 2001
66554	Freightliner. 2002*
66555–66566	Freightliner. 2002
66567–66574	Freightliner. 2003

66575–66577	Freightliner. 2004
66578–66581	Freightliner. 2005
66582–66594	Freightliner. 2007 (66582/583/584/586 exported to Poland).
66595–66599	Freightliner. 2008
66601–66606	Freightliner. 2000
66607–66612	Freightliner. 2002
66613–66618	Freightliner. 2003
66619–66622	Freightliner. 2005
66623–66625	Freightliner. 2007 (66624/625 exported to Poland).
66701–66707	GB Railfreight. 2001
66708–66712	GB Railfreight. 2002
66713–66717	GB Railfreight. 2003
66718–66722	GB Railfreight. 2006
66723–66727	GB Railfreight. 2006
66728–66732	GB Railfreight. 2008
66951–66952	Freightliner. 2004
66953–66957	Freightliner. 2008

* Replacement for 66521, written off in the Great Heck accident in 2001.

Class 66/0. DB Schenker-operated locomotives.

All fitted with Swinghead Automatic "Buckeye" Combination Couplers except 66001 and 66002.

† Fitted with additional lights and drawgear for Lickey banking duties.

66001	E	A	WBST	TO	
66002	E	A	WFMU	TO	Lafarge Quorn
66003	E	A	WFMU	TO	
66004	E	A	WFMU	TO	
66005	E	A	WFMU	TO	
66006	E	A	WFMU	TO	
66007	E	A	WFMU	TO	
66008	E	A	WFMU	TO	
66009	E	A	WFMU	TO	
66010	E	A	WBES	TO	
66011	E	A	WFMU	TO	
66012	E	A	WFMU	TO	
66013	E	A	WFMU	TO	
66014	E	A	WFMU	TO	
66015	E	A	WFMU	TO	
66016	E	A	WBSN	TO	
66017	E	A	WBST	TO	
66018	E	A	WFMU	TO	
66019	E	A	WBST	TO	
66020	E	A	WFMU	TO	
66021	E	A	WFMU	TO	
66023	E	A	WFMU	TO	
66024	E	A	WFMU	TO	
66025	E	A	WFMU	TO	
66026	E	A	WBES	TO	
66027	E	A	WFMU	TO	
66028	E	A	WBES	TO	

66029	E	A	WBES	TO	
66030	E	A	WFMU	TO	
66031	E	A	WFMU	TO	
66033	E	A	WBES	TO	
66034	E	A	WFMU	TO	
66035	E	A	WFMU	TO	
66037	E	A	WFMU	TO	
66039	E	A	WFMU	TO	
66040	E	A	WFMU	TO	
66041	E	A	WFMU	TO	
66042	E	A	WBES	TO	
66043	E	A	WFMU	TO	
66044	E	A	WFMU	TO	
66046	E	A	WFMU	TO	
66047	E	A	WFMU	TO	
66048	AL	A	WFMU	TO (S)	James the Engine
66050	E	A	WFMU	TO	EWS Energy
66051	E	A	WFMU	TO	
66053	E	A	WFMU	TO	
66054	E	A	WFMU	TO	
66055 †	E	A	WFMU	TO	
66056 †	E	A	WFMU	TO	
66057 †	E	A	WFMU	TO	
66058 †	E	A	WFMU	TO	
66059 †	E	A	WFMU	TO	
66060	E	A	WFMU	TO	
66061	E	A	WFMU	TO	
66062	E	A	WBES	TO	
66063	E	A	WFMU	TO	
66065	E	A	WFMU	TO	
66066	E	A	WFMU	TO	
66067	E	A	WFMU	TO	
66068	E	A	WFMU	TO	
66069	E	A	WFMU	TO	
66070	E	A	WFMU	TO	
66071	E	A	WBES	TO	
66072	E	A	WBES	TO	
66073	E	A	WBES	TO	
66074	E	A	WFMU	TO	
66075	E	A	WFMU	TO	
66076	E	A	WFMU	TO	
66077	E	A	WBSN	TO	Benjamin Gimbert G.C.
66078	E	A	WFMU	TO	
66079	E	A	WFMU	TO	James Nightall G.C.
66080	E	A	WFMU	TO	
66081	E	A	WFMU	TO	
66082	E	A	WFMU	TO	
66083	E	A	WFMU	TO	
66084	E	A	WFMU	TO	
66085	E	A	WFMU	TO	
66086	E	A	WFMU	TO	

66087	**E**	A	WFMU	TO
66088	**E**	A	WFMU	TO
66089	**E**	A	WFMU	TO
66090	**E**	A	WFMU	TO
66091	**E**	A	WFMU	TO
66092	**E**	A	WFMU	TO
66093	**E**	A	WFMU	TO
66094	**E**	A	WFMU	TO
66095	**E**	A	WFMU	TO
66096	**E**	A	WFMU	TO
66097	**E**	A	WFMU	TO
66098	**E**	A	WFMU	TO
66099 r	**E**	A	WFMU	TO
66100 r	**E**	A	WFMU	TO
66101 r	**E**	A	WFMU	TO
66102 r	**E**	A	WFMU	TO
66103 r	**E**	A	WFMU	TO
66104 r	**E**	A	WFMU	TO
66105 r	**E**	A	WBSN	TO
66106 r	**E**	A	WFMU	TO
66107 r	**E**	A	WFMU	TO
66108 r	**E**	A	WBSN	TO
66109	**E**	A	WFMU	TO
66110 r	**E**	A	WFMU	TO
66111 r	**E**	A	WFMU	TO
66112 r	**E**	A	WFMU	TO
66113 r	**E**	A	WFMU	TO
66114 r	**E**	A	WFMU	TO
66115	**E**	A	WFMU	TO
66116	**E**	A	WFMU	TO
66117	**E**	A	WFMU	TO
66118	**E**	A	WFMU	TO
66119	**E**	A	WFMU	TO
66120	**E**	A	WFMU	TO
66121	**E**	A	WFMU	TO
66122	**E**	A	WFMU	TO
66123	**E**	A	WBES	TO
66124	**E**	A	WFMU	TO
66125	**E**	A	WFMU	TO
66126	**E**	A	WFMU	TO
66127	**E**	A	WFMU	TO
66128	**E**	A	WFMU	TO
66129	**E**	A	WFMU	TO
66130	**E**	A	WBSN	TO
66131	**E**	A	WFMU	TO
66132	**E**	A	WFMU	TO
66133	**E**	A	WFMU	TO
66134	**E**	A	WFMU	TO
66135	**E**	A	WFMU	TO
66136	**E**	A	WFMU	TO
66137	**E**	A	WFMU	TO

66138	E	A	WFMU	TO	
66139	E	A	WFMU	TO	
66140	E	A	WFMU	TO	
66141	E	A	WFMU	TO	
66142	E	A	WFMU	TO	
66143	E	A	WFMU	TO	
66144	E	A	WFMU	TO	
66145	E	A	WFMU	TO	
66146	E	A	WFMU	TO	
66147	E	A	WFMU	TO	
66148	E	A	WFMU	TO	
66149	E	A	WFMU	TO	
66150	E	A	WFMU	TO	
66151	E	A	WFMU	TO	
66152	DB	A	WFMU	TO	Derek Holmes Railway Operator
66153	E	A	WFMU	TO	
66154	E	A	WFMU	TO	
66155	E	A	WFMU	TO	
66156	E	A	WFMU	TO	
66157	E	A	WFMU	TO	
66158	E	A	WFMU	TO	
66159	E	A	WFMU	TO	
66160	E	A	WFMU	TO	
66161	E	A	WFMU	TO	
66162	E	A	WFMU	TO	
66163	E	A	WFMU	TO	
66164	E	A	WFMU	TO	
66165	E	A	WFMU	TO	
66166	E	A	WFMU	TO	
66167	E	A	WBSN	TO	
66168	E	A	WFMU	TO	
66169	E	A	WFMU	TO	
66170	E	A	WFMU	TO	
66171	E	A	WFMU	TO	
66172	E	A	WFMU	TO	PAUL MELLENEY
66173	E	A	WFMU	TO	
66174	E	A	WFMU	TO	
66175	E	A	WFMU	TO	
66176	E	A	WFMU	TO	
66177	E	A	WFMU	TO	
66178	E	A	WFMU	TO	
66180	E	A	WFMU	TO	
66181	E	A	WFMU	TO	
66182	E	A	WFMU	TO	
66183	E	A	WFMU	TO	
66184	E	A	WFMU	TO	
66185	E	A	WFMU	TO	
66186	E	A	WFMU	TO	
66187	E	A	WFMU	TO	
66188	E	A	WFMU	TO	
66189	E	A	WFMU	TO	

66191	**E**	A	WBES	TO
66192	**E**	A	WFMU	TO
66193	**E**	A	WNTR	TO
66194	**E**	A	WFMU	TO
66196	**E**	A	WFMU	TO
66197	**E**	A	WFMU	TO
66198	**E**	A	WFMU	TO
66199	**E**	A	WFMU	TO
66200	**E**	A	WFMU	TO
66201	**E**	A	WFMU	TO
66204	**E**	A	WFMU	TO
66206	**E**	A	WFMU	TO
66207	**E**	A	WBSN	TO
66213	**E**	A	WFMU	TO
66221	**E**	A	WFMU	TO
66227	**E**	A	WFMU	TO
66230	**E**	A	WFMU	TO
66232	**E**	A	WFMU	TO
66237	**E**	A	WFMU	TO
66238	**E**	A	WFMU	TO
66239	**E**	A	WBES	TO
66243	**E**	A	WBES	TO
66248	**E**	A	WFMU	TO
66249	**E**	A	WBES	TO
66250	**E**	A	WFMU	TO

RAILWAY HERITAGE COMMITTEE

Class 66/3. Former Fastline-operated locomotives. Low emission. Details as Class 66/0 except:

Engine: EMD 12N-710G3B-U2 two stroke of 2420 kW (3245 h.p.) at 904 r.p.m.
Traction Motors: General Motors D43TRC.
Fuel Capacity: 5150 litres.

66301	**FA**	BN	MBDL	CR (S)
66302	**FA**	BN	MBDL	CR (S)
66303	**FA**	BN	MBDL	CR (S)
66304	**FA**	BN	MBDL	KM (S)
66305	**FA**	BN	MBDL	CR (S)

Class 66/4. Former Direct Rail Services-operated locomotives.
66401–66405. Porterbrook spot-hire locos. Details as Class 66/0.

66401	**DS**	P	GBRT	WB
66402	**DS**	P	GBRT	WB
66403	**DS**	P	GBRT	WB
66404	**DS**	P	GBRT	WB
66405	**DS**	P	GBRT	WB

66411–66434. Low emission. HBOS-owned. Details as Class 66/0 except:

Engine: EMD 12N-710G3B-U2 two stroke of 2420 kW (3245 h.p.) at 904 r.p.m.
Traction Motors: General Motors D43TRC.
Fuel Capacity: 5150 litres.

Advertising liveries: 66411 & 66414 Stobart Rail (two tone blue & white).
66412 Malcolm Rail (black with a red solebar stripe).

66411	**AL**	HX	XHIM	KM	Eddie the Engine
66412	**AL**	HX	XHIM	KM	
66413	**DS**	HX	XHIM	KM	
66414	**AL**	HX	XHIM	KM	James the Engine
66415	**DS**	HX	XHIM	KM	
66416	**DS**	HX	XHIM	KM	
66417	**DS**	HX	XHIM	KM	
66418	**DS**	HX	XHIM	KM	
66419	**DS**	HX	XHIM	KM	
66420	**DS**	HX	XHIM	KM	
66421	**DS**	HX	XHIM	KM	
66422	**DS**	HX	XHIM	KM	
66423	**DS**	HX	XHIM	KM	
66424	**DS**	HX	XHIM	KM	
66425	**DS**	HX	XHIM	KM	
66426	**DS**	HX	XHIM	KM	
66427	**DS**	HX	XHIM	KM	
66428	**DS**	HX	XHIM	KM	
66429	**DS**	HX	XHIM	KM	
66430	**DS**	HX	XHIM	KM	
66431	**DS**	HX	XHIM	KM	
66432	**DS**	HX	XHIM	KM	
66433	**DS**	HX	XHIM	KM	
66434	**FA**	HX	XHIM	KM	

Class 66/5. Freightliner-operated locomotives. Details as Class 66/0.

Advertising livery: 66522 Shanks Waste (one half of loco Freightliner green and one half Shanks' Waste light green).

66501	**FL**	P	DFGM	FD	Japan 2001
66502	**FL**	P	DFGM	FD	Basford Hall Centenary 2001
66503	**FL**	P	DFGM	FD	The RAILWAY MAGAZINE
66504	**FL**	P	DFGM	FD	
66505	**FL**	P	DFGM	FD	
66506	**FL**	E	DFHH	FD	Crewe Regeneration
66507	**FL**	E	DFTZ	LD	
66508	**FL**	E	DFRT	FD	
66509	**FL**	E	DFHH	FD	
66510	**FL**	E	DFRT	FD	
66511	**FL**	E	DFRT	FD	
66512	**FL**	E	DFHH	FD	
66513	**FL**	E	DFHH	FD	
66514	**FL**	E	DFRT	FD	
66515	**FL**	E	DFRT	FD	
66516	**FL**	E	DFGM	FD	
66517	**FL**	E	DFGM	FD	
66518	**FL**	E	DFRT	FD	
66519	**FL**	E	DFHH	FD	
66520	**FL**	E	DFRT	FD	

66522	**AL**	E	DFRT	LD	
66523	**FL**	E	DFRT	FD	
66524	**FL**	E	DFHH	LD	
66525	**FL**	E	DFHH	FD	
66526	**FL**	P	DFRT	LD	Driver Steve Dunn (George)
66527	**FL**	P	DFRT	LD	Don Raider
66528	**FL**	P	DFHH	FD	
66529	**FL**	P	DFHH	FD	
66530	**FL**	P	DFHH	LD	
66531	**FL**	P	DFHH	FD	
66532	**FL**	P	DFGM	FD	P&O Nedlloyd Atlas
66533	**FL**	P	DFGM	FD	Hanjin Express/Senator Express
66534	**FL**	P	DFGM	FD	OOCL Express
66535	**FL**	P	DFGM	FD	
66536	**FL**	P	DFGM	FD	
66537	**FL**	P	DFGM	FD	
66538	**FL**	E	DFIM	FD	
66539	**FL**	E	DFIM	FD	
66540	**FL**	E	DFIM	FD	Ruby
66541	**FL**	E	DFIM	FD	
66542	**FL**	E	DFIM	FD	
66543	**FL**	E	DFIM	FD	
66544	**FL**	P	DFTZ	LD	
66545	**FL**	P	DFHG	FD	
66546	**FL**	P	DFTZ	LD	
66547	**FL**	P	DFTZ	BA	
66548	**FL**	P	DFHG	LD	
66549	**FL**	P	DFHG	LD	
66550	**FL**	P	DFHG	LD	
66551	**FL**	P	DFTZ	BA	
66552	**FL**	P	DFTZ	BA	Maltby Raider
66553	**FL**	P	DFHG	LD	
66554	**FL**	E	DFHG	LD	
66555	**FL**	E	DFHG	LD	
66556	**FL**	E	DFHG	LD	
66557	**FL**	E	DFHG	FD	
66558	**FL**	E	DFHG	FD	
66559	**FL**	E	DFHG	LD	
66560	**FL**	E	DFHG	FD	
66561	**FL**	E	DFHG	FD	
66562	**FL**	E	DFIM	LD	
66563	**FL**	E	DFIM	FD	
66564	**FL**	E	DFIM	LD	
66565	**FL**	E	DFIM	LD	
66566	**FL**	E	DFIM	LD	
66567	**FL**	E	DFIM	FD	
66568	**FL**	E	DFIM	FD	
66569	**FL**	E	DFIM	FD	
66570	**FL**	E	DFIM	FD	
66571	**FL**	E	DFIM	FD	
66572	**FL**	E	DFIM	FD	

66573	**FL**	E	DFTZ	Dagenham	
66574	**FL**	E	DFTZ	Dagenham	
66575	**FL**	E	DFIM	FD	
66576	**FL**	E	DFIM	FD	Hamburg Sud Advantage
66577	**FL**	E	DFIM	FD	
66578	**FL**	E	DFTZ	LD	
66579	**FL**	E	DFTZ	LD	
66580	**FL**	E	DFTZ	SZ	
66581	**FL**	E	DFTZ	SZ	

Class 66/5. Freightliner-operated low emission locos. Details as Class 66/0 except:

Engine: EMD 12N-710G3B-U2 two stroke of 2420 kW (3245 h.p.) at 904 r.p.m.
Traction Motors: General Motors D43TRC.
Fuel Capacity: 5150 litres.

66585	**FL**	HX	DFHG	FD	The Drax Flyer
66587	**FL**	HX	DFIN	FD	
66588	**FL**	HX	DFIN	FD	
66589	**FL**	HX	DFIN	FD	
66590	**FL**	HX	DFIN	FD	
66591	**FL**	LY	DFIN	FD	
66592	**FL**	LY	DFIN	FD	Johnson Stevens Agencies
66593	**FL**	LY	DFIN	FD	3MG MERSEY MULTIMODAL GATEWAY
66594	**FL**	LY	DFIN	FD	NYK Spirit of Kyoto
66595	**FL**	BN	DFHG	FD	
66596	**FL**	BN	DFHG	FD	
66597	**FL**	BN	DFHG	FD	
66598	**FL**	BN	DFHG	FD	
66599	**FL**	BN	DFHG	FD	

Class 66/6. Freightliner-operated locomotives with modified gear ratios. Details as Class 66/0 except:

Maximum Tractive Effort: 467 kN (105080 lbf).
Continuous Tractive Effort: 296 kN (66630 lbf) at 14.0 m.p.h.
Design Speed: 65 m.p.h.   **Maximum Speed:** 65 m.p.h.

66601	**FL**	P	DFHH	LD	The Hope Valley
66602	**FL**	P	DFRT	FD	
66603	**FL**	P	DFRT	FD	
66604	**FL**	P	DFRT	FD	
66605	**FL**	P	DFRT	FD	
66606	**FL**	P	DFRT	FD	
66607	**FL**	P	DFHG	FD	
66608	**FL**	P	DFHG	FD	
66609	**FL**	P	DFHG	FD	
66610	**FL**	P	DFHG	FD	
66611	**FL**	P	DFHG	FD	
66612	**FL**	P	DFHG	FD	Forth Raider
66613	**FL**	E	DFTZ	BA	
66614	**FL**	E	DFHG	FD	
66615	**FL**	E	DFHG	FD	

66616	**FL**	E	DFHG	FD
66617	**FL**	E	DFHG	FD
66618	**FL**	E	DFHG	FD

Railways Illustrated Annual
Photographic Awards Alan Barnes
Derek W. Johnson MBE

66619	**FL**	E	DFHG	FD
66620	**FL**	E	DFHG	FD
66621	**FL**	E	DFHG	FD
66622	**FL**	E	DFHG	FD

Class 66/6. Freightliner-operated low emission loco with modified gear ratios.
Fuel Capacity: 5150 litres.

Advertising livery: 66623 Bardon Aggregates (blue).

| 66623 | **AL** | HX | DFHG | FD | Bill Bolsover |

Class 66/7. First GBRf-operated locomotives. Details as Class 66/0.

Non-standard/Advertising liveries:

66705 **GB** livery but with the addition of "Union Jack" bodyside vinyls.
66709 Black & orange with MEDITE branding.

66701	**GB**	E	GBCM	WB	Whitemoor
66702	**GB**	E	GBCM	WB	Blue Lightning
66703	**GB**	E	GBCM	WB	Doncaster PSB 1981–2002
66704	**GB**	E	GBCM	WB	Colchester Power Signalbox
66705	**GB**	E	GBCM	WB	Golden Jubilee
66706	**GB**	E	GBCM	WB	Nene Valley
66707	**GB**	E	GBCM	WB	Sir Sam Fay GREAT CENTRAL RAILWAY
66708	**GB**	E	GBCM	WB	
66709	**AL**	E	GBCM	WB	Joseph Arnold Davies
66710	**GB**	E	GBCM	WB	
66711	**GB**	E	GBCM	WB	
66712	**GB**	E	GBCM	WB	Peterborough Power Signalbox
66713	**GB**	E	GBCM	WB	Forest City
66714	**GB**	E	GBCM	WB	Cromer Lifeboat
66715	**GB**	E	GBCM	WB	VALOUR – IN MEMORY OF ALL RAILWAY EMPLOYEES WHO GAVE THEIR LIVES FOR THEIR COUNTRY
66716	**GB**	E	GBCM	WB	
66717	**GB**	E	GBCM	WB	Good Old Boy

66718–66732. Low emission. Details as Class 66/0 except:

Engine: EMD 12N-710G3B-U2 two stroke of 2420 kW (3245 h.p.) at 904 r.p.m.
Traction Motors: General Motors D43TRC.
Fuel Capacity: 5546 litres (66718–722) or 5150 litres (66723–732).

66718	**MT**	E	GBCM	WB	Gwyneth Dunwoody
66719	**MT**	E	GBCM	WB	METRO-LAND
66720	**MT**	E	GBCM	WB	Metronet Pathfinder
66721	**MT**	E	GBCM	WB	Harry Beck
66722	**MT**	E	GBCM	WB	Sir Edward Watkin
66723 r	**FS**	E	GBSD	WB	Chinook
66724 r	**FS**	E	GBSD	WB	Drax Power Station

66725	r	**FS**	E	GBSD	WB	SUNDERLAND
66726	r	**FS**	E	GBSD	WB	SHEFFIELD WEDNESDAY
66727	r	**FS**	E	GBSD	WB	Andrew Scott CBE
66728		**FS**	P	GBMU	WB	Institution of Railway Operators
66729		**FS**	P	GBMU	WB	DERBY COUNTY
66730		**FS**	P	GBMU	WB	
66731		**FS**	P	GBMU	WB	
66732		**FS**	P	GBMU	WB	GBRf The First Decade 1999–2009
						John Smith – MD

Class 66/8. Former DRS Class 66/4s originally overhauled for Advenza Freight. Now used by Colas Rail. Details as Class 66/0:

66841	(66406)	**CS**	P	COLO	FD
66842	(66407)	**CS**	P	COLO	FD
66843	(66408)	**CS**	P	COLO	FD
66844	(66409)	**CS**	P	COLO	FD
66845	(66410)	**DS**	P	COLO	FD

Class 66/9. Freightliner locos. Low emission "demonstrator" locos. Details as Class 66/0 except:

Engine: EMD 12N-710G3B-U2 two stroke of 2420 kW (3245 h.p.) at 904 r.p.m.
Traction Motors: General Motors D43TRC.
Fuel Capacity: 5905/5150 litres.

| 66951 | **FL** | E | DFHG | FD |
| 66952 | **FL** | E | DFHG | FD |

Class 66/9. Freightliner-operated low emission locos. Due to the 665xx number range being full further orders of 66/5s are to be numbered from 66953 onwards. Details as Class 66/5 (low emission):

66953	**FL**	BN	DFHG	FD
66954	**FL**	BN	DFIN	FD
66955	**FL**	BN	DFIN	FD
66956	**FL**	BN	DFIN	FD
66957	**FL**	BN	DFHG	FD	Stephenson Locomotive Society 1909–2009

CLASS 67 ALSTOM/GENERAL MOTORS EMD Bo-Bo

Built: 1999–2000 by Alstom at Valencia, Spain, as sub-contractors for General Motors (General Motors model JT42 HW-HS).
Engine: GM 12N-710G3B-EC two stroke of 2385 kW (3200 h.p.) at 904 r.p.m.
Main Alternator: General Motors AR9A/HEP7/CA6C.
Traction Motors: General Motors D43FM.
Maximum Tractive Effort: 141 kN (31770 lbf).
Continuous Tractive Effort: 90 kN (20200 lbf) at 46.5 m.p.h.
Power At Rail: 1860 kW.   **Train Brakes:** Air.
Brake Force: 78 t.   **Dimensions:** 19.74 x 2.72 m.
Weight: 90 t.   **Wheel Diameter:** 965 mm.
Design Speed: 125 m.p.h.
Maximum Speed: 125 m.p.h. (but only currently authorised for 110 m.p.h.)

Fuel Capacity: 4927 litres.   **RA:** 8.
Train Supply: Electric, index 66.   **Multiple Working:** AAR System.

Notes: All equipped with Slow Speed Control and Swinghead Automatic "Buckeye" Combination Couplers.

67004, 67007, 67009, 67011 and 67030 are fitted with cast iron brake blocks for working the Fort William Sleeper. **Maximum Speed:** 80 m.p.h.

67002, 67004 and 67027 carry their names on one side only.

Non-standard livery: 67029 All over silver with EWS logos (EWS "Special Train").

67001	**E**	A	WNTR	TO	
67002	**E**	A	WAAN	CE	Special Delivery
67003	**E**	A	WAAN	CE	
67004 r	**E**	A	WABN	CE	Post Haste
67005	**RZ**	A	WAAN	CE	Queen's Messenger
67006	**RZ**	A	WAAN	CE	Royal Sovereign
67007 r	**E**	A	WABN	CE	
67008	**E**	A	WAAN	CE	
67009 r	**E**	A	WABN	CE	
67010	**WS**	A	WNTR	TO	
67011 r	**E**	A	WABN	CE	
67012	**WS**	A	WAWN	CE	A Shropshire Lad
67013	**WS**	A	WAWN	CE	Dyfrbont Pontcysyllte
67014	**WS**	A	WAWN	CE	Thomas Telford
67015	**WS**	A	WAWN	CE	David J. Lloyd
67016	**E**	A	WAFN	CE	
67017	**E**	A	WAFN	CE	Arrow
67018	**DB**	A	WAAN	CE	Keith Heller
67019	**E**	A	WAFN	CE	
67020	**E**	A	WAAN	CE	
67021	**E**	A	WAAN	CE	
67022	**E**	A	WAAN	CE	
67023	**E**	A	WAAN	CE	
67024	**E**	A	WAAN	CE	
67025	**E**	A	WAAN	CE	Western Star
67026	**E**	A	WAAN	CE	
67027	**E**	A	WAFN	CE	Rising Star
67028	**E**	A	WAAN	CE	
67029	**O**	A	WAAN	CE	Royal Diamond
67030 r	**E**	A	WABN	CE	

CLASS 70   GENERAL ELECTRIC   Co-Co

30 new General Electric "PowerHaul" locos are currently being delivered to Freightliner. The first six locos arrived in the UK in late 2009, but the remaining 24 locos are due to arrive over a protracted period, with 70007–012 due to arrive autumn 2010.

Built: 2009–2011 by General Electric, Erie, Pennsylvania, USA.
Engine: General Electric PowerHaul P616 of 2750 kW (3700 h.p.) at 904 r.p.m.
Main Alternator: General Electric GTA series.
Traction Motors: AC-GE 5GEB30.
Maximum Tractive Effort: 544 kN (122 000 lbf).
Continuous Tractive Effort: 427 kN (96 000 lbf) at ?? m.p.h.

Power At Rail:	**Train Brakes:** Air.
Brake Force: 97.6 t.	**Dimensions:** 21.71 x 2.64 m.
Weight: 129 t.	**Wheel Diameter:** 1007 mm.
Design Speed: 75 m.p.h.	**Maximum Speed:** 75 m.p.h.
Fuel Capacity: 6000 litres.	**RA:** 7.
Train Supply: Not equipped.	**Multiple Working:** Within class.

70001	**FH**	LY	DFGI	LD	PowerHaul
70002	**FH**	LY	DFGH	LD	
70003	**FH**	LY	DFGH	LD	
70004	**FH**	LY	DFGH	LD	
70005	**FH**	LY	DFGH	LD	
70006	**FH**	LY	DFGH	LD	
70007	**FH**	LY			
70008	**FH**	LY			
70009	**FH**	LY			
70010	**FH**	LY			
70011	**FH**	LY			
70012	**FH**	LY			
70013					
70014					
70015					
70016					
70017					
70018					
70019					
70020					
70021					
70022					
70023					
70024					
70025					
70026					
70027					
70028					
70029					
70030					

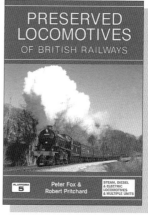

2. ELECTRO-DIESEL & ELECTRIC LOCOMOTIVES

CLASS 73   BR/ENGLISH ELECTRIC   Bo-Bo

Electro-diesel locomotives which can operate either from a DC supply or using power from a diesel engine.

Built: 1965–1967 by English Electric Co. at Vulcan Foundry, Newton-le-Willows.
Engine: English Electric 4SRKT of 447 kW (600 h.p.) at 850 r.p.m.
Main Generator: English Electric 824/5D.
Electric Supply System: 750 V DC from third rail.
Traction Motors: English Electric 546/1B.
Maximum Tractive Effort (Electric): 179 kN (40000 lbf).
Maximum Tractive Effort (Diesel): 160 kN (36000 lbf).
Continuous Rating (Electric): 1060 kW (1420 h.p.) giving a tractive effort of 35 kN (7800 lbf) at 68 m.p.h.
Continuous Tractive Effort (Diesel): 60 kN (13600 lbf) at 11.5 m.p.h.
Maximum Rail Power (Electric): 2350 kW (3150 h.p.) at 42 m.p.h.
Train Brakes: Air, vacuum & electro-pneumatic († Air & electro-pneumatic).
Brake Force: 31 t.   **Dimensions:** 16.36 x 2.64 m.
Weight: 77 t.   **Wheel Diameter:** 1016 mm.
Design Speed: 90 m.p.h.   **Maximum Speed:** 90 m.p.h.
Fuel Capacity: 1409 litres.   **RA:** 6.
Train Supply: Electric, index 66 (on electric power only).
Multiple Working: SR 27-way System & Blue Star.

Formerly numbered E6001–E6020/E6022–E6026/E6028–E6049 (not in order).

Note: Locomotives numbered in the 732xx series are classed as 73/2 and were originally dedicated to Gatwick Express services.

Non-standard livery: 73107 Two-tone grey.

73107	**0**	20	MBED	SE	Redhill 1844–1994
73109	**SD**	TT	MBED	SL	Battle of Britain 50th Anniversary
73133	**TT**	TT	MBED	SU	
73136	**TT**	TT	MBED	SU	
73138	**Y**	NR	QADD	ZA	
73141	**FS**	GB	GBED	SE	Charlotte
73201 †	**B**	20	MBED	SE	Broadlands
73202 †	**GV**	P	IVGA	SL	Dave Berry
73204 †	**GB**	GB	GBED	SE	Janice
73205 †	**GB**	GB	GBED	SE	Jeanette
73206 †	**GB**	GB	GBED	SE	Lisa
73207 †	**BL**	GB	GBED	SE	
73208 †	**B**	GB	GBED	SE	Kirsten
73209 †	**GB**	GB	GBZZ	SE	Alison
73211 †	**GX**	TT	MBED	SL (S)	
73212 †	**FS**	GB	GBED	SE	

73213	†	**FS**	GB	GBED	SE
73235	†	**SD**	P	HYWD	WD

CLASS 86   BR/ENGLISH ELECTRIC   Bo-Bo

Built: 1965–1966 by English Electric Co. at Vulcan Foundry, Newton-le-Willows or by BR at Doncaster Works.
Electric Supply System: 25 kV AC 50 Hz overhead.
Train Brakes: Air.
Dimensions: 17.83 x 2.65 m.
RA: 6.
Train Supply: Electric, index 66.
Brake Force: 40 t.
Weight: 83–86.8 t.
Multiple Working: TDM system.

Formerly numbered E3101–E3200 (not in order).

Class 86/1. Class 87-type bogies & motors.

Details as above except:
Traction Motors: GEC 412AZ frame mounted.
Maximum Tractive Effort: 258 kN (58000 lbf).
Continuous Rating: 3730 kW (5000 h.p.) giving a tractive effort of 95 kN (21300 lbf) at 87 m.p.h.
Maximum Rail Power: 5860 kW (7860 h.p.) at 50.8 m.p.h.
Wheel Diameter: 1150 mm.
Weight: 86.8 t.
Design Speed: 110 m.p.h.
Maximum Speed: 110 m.p.h.

86101	**B**	EL	ACAC	CP	Sir William A Stanier FRS

Class 86/2. Standard design rebuilt with resilient wheels and Flexicoil suspension.

Traction Motors: AEI 282BZ axle hung.
Maximum Tractive Effort: 207 kN (46500 lbf).
Continuous Rating: 3010 kW (4040 h.p.) giving a tractive effort of 85 kN (19200 lbf) at 77.5 m.p.h.
Maximum Rail Power: 4550 kW (6100 h.p.) at 49.5 m.p.h.
Wheel Diameter: 1156 mm.
Weight: 85–86.2 t.
Design Speed: 125 m.p.h.
Maximum Speed: 100 m.p.h.

Non-standard livery/numbering: 86233 & 86259 BR "Electric blue" livery. 86233 Also carries number E3172.

86212	**V**	E	SAXL	LM	
86213	**IC**	EL	ACXX	WB	Lancashire Witch
86215	**AR**	EP	EPXX	LM	
86217	**AR**	E	SAXL	LM	
86218	**AR**	E	SAXL	LM	
86223	**AR**	E	SAXL	LM	
86226	**V**	E	SAXL	LM	
86228	**IC**	E	SAXL	LM	
86229	**V**	E	SAXL	LM	
86230	**AR**	E	SAXL	LM	
86231	**V**	E	SAXL	LM	
86233	**O**	EP	EPXX	LM	

86234	**AR**	E	SAXL	LM	
86235	**AR**	E	SAXL	LM	
86242	**AR**	E	SAXL	LM	
86246	**AR**	E	SAXL	LM	
86247	**EL**	EP	EPXX	LM	
86251	**V**	E	SAXL	LM	
86259	**O**	LR	MBEL	TM	Les Ross

Class 86/4.

Traction Motors: AEI 282AZ axle hung.
Maximum Tractive Effort: 258 kN (58000 lbf).
Continuous Rating: 2680 kW (3600 h.p.) giving a tractive effort of 89 kN (20000 lbf) at 67 m.p.h.
Maximum Rail Power: 4400 kW (5900 h.p.) at 38 m.p.h.
Wheel Diameter: 1156 mm.   **Weight:** 83–83.9 t.
Design Speed: 100 m.p.h.   **Maximum Speed:** 100 m.p.h.

86401	**N**	EL	ACXX	WN	Northampton Town
86424	**Y**	NR	QSTR	CP	

Class 86/5. Regeared locomotive operated by Freightliner.

Details as Class 86/4 except:

Continuous Rating: 2680 kW (3600 h.p.) giving a tractive effort of 117 kN (26300 lbf) at 67 m.p.h.
Maximum Speed: 75 m.p.h.   **Train Supply:** Electric, isolated.

| 86501 (86608) | **FL** | FL | DFGC | FE |

Class 86/6. Freightliner-operated locomotives.

Details as Class 86/4 except:

Maximum Speed: 75 m.p.h.   **Train Supply:** Electric, isolated.

86604	**FL**	FL	DFNC	FE
86605	**FL**	FL	DFNC	FE
86607	**FL**	FL	DFNC	FE
86609	**FL**	FL	DFNC	FE
86610	**FL**	FL	DFNC	FE
86612	**FL**	P	DFNC	FE
86613	**FL**	P	DFNC	FE
86614	**FL**	P	DFNC	FE
86621	**FL**	P	DFNC	FE
86622	**FH**	P	DFNC	FE
86627	**FL**	P	DFNC	FE
86628	**FL**	P	DFNC	FE
86632	**FL**	P	DFNC	FE
86633	**FF**	P	DHLT	CP
86635	**FL**	P	DHLT	CP
86637	**FH**	P	DFNC	FE
86638	**FL**	P	DFNC	FE
86639	**FL**	P	DFNC	FE

Class 86/7. Europhoenix-owned locomotives. Refurbished Class 86/2s for the UK spot-hire market. Details as Class 86/2 unless stated.

Maximum Speed: 110 m.p.h.   **Weight:** 85 t.
Train Supply: Electric, index 74.

86701	(86205)	**EL**	EP	ETLO	CP	Orion
86702	(86260)	**EL**	EP	ETLO	CP	Cassiopeia

Class 86/9. Network Rail-owned locomotives. Rebuilt from Class 86/2s for use as Mobile Load Bank test locos to test Overhead Line Equipment, initially on the WCML. No. 1 end Traction Motors isolated. Can still move under own power.

Maximum Speed: 60 m.p.h.   **Train Supply:** Electric, isolated.

86901	(86253)	**Y**	NR	QACL	CP	CHIEF ENGINEER
86902	(86210)	**Y**	NR	QACL	CP	RAIL VEHICLE ENGINEERING

CLASS 87   BREL/GEC   Bo-Bo

Built: 1973–1975 by BREL at Crewe Works.
Electric Supply System: 25 kV AC 50 Hz overhead.
Traction Motors: GEC G412AZ frame mounted.
Maximum Tractive Effort: 258 kN (58000 lbf).
Continuous Rating: 3730 kW (5000 h.p.) giving a tractive effort of 95 kN (21300 lbf) at 87 m.p.h.
Maximum Rail Power: 5860 kW (7860 h.p.) at 50.8 m.p.h.
Train Brakes: Air.   **Brake Force:** 40 t.
Dimensions: 17.83 x 2.65 m.   **Weight:** 83.3 t.
Wheel Diameter: 1150 mm.   **Design Speed:** 110 m.p.h.
Maximum Speed: 110 m.p.h.   **Train Supply:** Electric, index 95.
RA: 6.   **Multiple Working:** TDM system.

87002	**B**	EL	ACAC	CP	Royal Sovereign
87009	**V**	X	SBXL	LM	
87017	**V**	X	SBXL	LM	
87021	**V**	X	SBXL	LM	
87023	**V**	X	SBXL	LM	
87025	**V**	X	SBXL	LM	
87027	**V**	X	SBXL	LM	

CLASS 90   GEC   Bo-Bo

Built: 1987–1990 by BREL at Crewe Works (as sub contractors for GEC).
Electric Supply System: 25 kV AC 50 Hz overhead.
Traction Motors: GEC G412CY frame mounted.
Maximum Tractive Effort: 258 kN (58000 lbf).
Continuous Rating: 3730 kW (5000 h.p.) giving a tractive effort of 95 kN (21300 lbf) at 87 m.p.h.
Maximum Rail Power: 5860 kW (7860 h.p.) at 68.3 m.p.h.
Train Brakes: Air.
Brake Force: 40 t.   **Dimensions:** 18.80 x 2.74 m.
Weight: 84.5 t.   **Wheel Diameter:** 1150 mm.
Design Speed: 110 m.p.h.   **Maximum Speed:** 110 m.p.h.
Train Supply: Electric, index 95.   **RA:** 7.
Multiple Working: TDM system.

Non-standard livery: 90036 As **FE** but with a yellow roof. EWS stickers.

90001	b	**1**	P	IANA	NC	
90002	b	**1**	P	IANA	NC	
90003	b	**NX**	P	IANA	NC	Rædwald of East Anglia
90004	b	**1**	P	IANA	NC	
90005	b	**1**	P	IANA	NC	Vice-Admiral Lord Nelson
90006	b	**1**	P	IANA	NC	Modern Railways Magazine/ Roger Ford
90007	b	**1**	P	IANA	NC	Sir John Betjeman
90008	b	**NX**	P	IANA	NC	
90009	b	**1**	P	IANA	NC	
90010	b	**1**	P	IANA	NC	
90011	b	**1**	P	IANA	NC	Let's Go East of England
90012	b	**1**	P	IANA	NC	Royal Anglian Regiment
90013	b	**1**	P	IANA	NC	The Evening Star PRIDE OF IPSWICH 1885–2010 125 YEARS OF SERVING SUFFOLK
90014	b	**1**	P	IANA	NC	Norfolk and Norwich Festival
90015	b	**NX**	P	IANA	NC	Colchester Castle
90016		**FL**	P	DFLC	FE	
90017	b	**E**	DB	WNTS	CE	
90018	b	**E**	DB	WEFE	CE	
90019	b	**FS**	DB	WEFE	CE	
90020	b	**E**	DB	WEFE	CE	Collingwood
90021		**FS**	DB	WEFE	CE	
90022		**EG**	DB	WNTS	CE	Freightconnection
90023		**E**	DB	WNTS	CE	
90024		**FS**	DB	WEFE	CE	
90025		**F**	DB	WNTS	CE	
90026		**E**	DB	WEFE	CE	
90027		**F**	DB	WNTS	CE	Allerton T&RS Depot
90028		**E**	DB	WNTS	CE	
90029		**E**	DB	WEFE	CE	The Institution of Civil Engineers
90030		**E**	DB	WNTS	CE	Crewe Locomotive Works

90031	E	DB	WNTS	CE	The Railway Children Partnership Working For Street Children Worldwide
90032	E	DB	WNTS	CE	
90033	FE	DB	WNTS	CE	
90034	E	DB	WNTS	CE	
90035	E	DB	WEFE	CE	
90036	O	DB	WEFE	CE	
90037	E	DB	WNTS	CE	Spirit of Dagenham
90038	FE	DB	WNTS	CE	
90039	E	DB	WEFE	CE	
90040	E	DB	WNTS	CE	The Railway Mission
90041	FL	P	DFLC	FE	
90042	FF	P	DFLC	FE	
90043	FF	P	DFLC	FE	Freightliner Coatbridge
90044	FF	P	DFLC	FE	
90045	FH	P	DFLC	FE	
90046	FL	P	DFLC	FE	
90047	FF	P	DFLC	FE	
90048	FH	P	DFLC	FE	
90049	FH	P	DFLC	FE	
90050	FF	DB	WNTS	CE	

CLASS 91   GEC   Bo-Bo

Built: 1988–1991 by BREL at Crewe Works (as sub contractors for GEC).
Electric Supply System: 25 kV AC 50 Hz overhead.
Traction Motors: GEC G426AZ.
Maximum Tractive Effort: 190 kN (43 000 lbf).
Continuous Rating: 4540 kW (6090 h.p.) giving a tractive effort of 170 kN at 96 m.p.h.
Maximum Rail Power: 4700 kW (6300 h.p.) at ?? m.p.h.
Train Brakes: Air.
Brake Force: 45 t.
Weight: 84 t.
Design Speed: 140 m.p.h.
Train Supply: Electric, index 95.
Multiple Working: TDM system.
Dimensions: 19.41 x 2.74 m.
Wheel Diameter: 1000 mm.
Maximum Speed: 125 m.p.h.
RA: 7.

Note: Locos originally numbered in the 910xx series, but renumbered upon completion of overhauls at Bombardier, Doncaster by the addition of 100 to their original number. The exception to this rule was 91023 which was renumbered 91132.

91101	EC	E	IECA	BN
91102	GN	E	IECA	BN
91103	GN	E	IECA	BN
91104	GN	E	IECA	BN
91105	GN	E	IECA	BN
91106	GN	E	IECA	BN
91107	EC	E	IECA	BN
91108	GN	E	IECA	BN

91109	**GN**	E	IECA	BN
91110	**GN**	E	IECA	BN
91111	**NX**	E	IECA	BN
91112	**GN**	E	IECA	BN
91113	**GN**	E	IECA	BN
91114	**GN**	E	IECA	BN
91115	**GN**	E	IECA	BN
91116	**GN**	E	IECA	BN
91117	**GN**	E	IECA	BN
91118	**GN**	E	IECA	BN
91119	**GN**	E	IECA	BN
91120	**GN**	E	IECA	BN
91121	**GN**	E	IECA	BN
91122	**GN**	E	IECA	BN
91124	**GN**	E	IECA	BN
91125	**GN**	E	IECA	BN
91126	**GN**	E	IECA	BN
91127	**GN**	E	IECA	BN
91128	**GN**	E	IECA	BN
91129	**GN**	E	IECA	BN
91130	**GN**	E	IECA	BN
91131	**GN**	E	IECA	BN
91132	**GN**	E	IECA	BN

CLASS 92   BRUSH   Co-Co

Built: 1993–1996 by Brush Traction at Loughborough.
Electric Supply System: 25 kV AC 50 Hz overhead or 750 V DC third rail.
Traction Motors: Asea Brown Boveri design. Model 6FRA 7059B (Asynchronous 3-phase induction motors).
Maximum Tractive Effort: 400 kN (90 000 lbf).
Continuous Rating: 5040 kW (6760 h.p.) on AC, 4000 kW (5360 h.p.) on DC.
Maximum Rail Power: **Train Brakes:** Air.
Brake Force: 63 t.   **Dimensions:** 21.34 x 2.67 m.
Weight: 126 t.   **Wheel Diameter:** 1070 mm.
Design Speed: 140 km/h (87 m.p.h.).   **Maximum Speed:** 145 km/h (90 m.p.h.).
Train Supply: Electric, index 108 (AC), 70 (DC).
RA: 7.

Advertising livery: 92017 Stobart Rail (two tone blue & white).

92001	**E**	HX	WTAE	CE	Victor Hugo
92002	**EG**	HX	WNTS	CE	H.G. Wells
92003	**EG**	HX	WTAE	CE	Beethoven
92004	**EG**	HX	WNTS	CE	Jane Austen
92005	**EG**	HX	WTAE	CE	Mozart
92006	**EP**	SF	WNWX	CE	Louis Armand
92007	**EG**	HX	WTAE	CE	Schubert
92008	**EG**	HX	WNTS	CE	Jules Verne
92009	**EG**	HX	WTAE	CE	Elgar
92010	**EP**	ET	PTXX	CO	Molière

92011	EG	HX	WNTS	CE	Handel
92012	EG	HX	WTAE	CE	Thomas Hardy
92013	EG	HX	WNTS	CE	Puccini
92014	EP	SF	WNWX	CE	Emile Zola
92015	EG	HX	WNTS	CE	D.H. Lawrence
92016	EG	HX	WNTR	CE	Brahms
92017	AL	HX	WTAE	CE	Bart the Engine
92018	EP	SF	WNWX	CE	Stendhal
92019	EG	HX	WTAE	CE	Wagner
92020	EP	ET	PTXX	LB (S)	Milton
92021	EP	ET	PTXX	LB (S)	Purcell
92022	EG	HX	WTAE	CE	Charles Dickens
92023	EP	SF	WNWX	CE	Ravel
92024	EG	IIX	WNTS	CE	J.S. Bach
92025	EG	HX	WNTS	CE	Oscar Wilde
92026	EG	HX	WTAE	CE	Britten
92027	EG	HX	WNTS	CE	George Eliot
92028	EP	ET	GBET	CO	Saint Saëns
92029	EG	HX	WNTS	CE	Dante
92030	EG	HX	WNTR	CE	Ashford
92031	E	HX	WTAE	CE	The Institute of Logistics and Transport
92032	EP	ET	GBET	CO	César Franck
92033	EP	SF	WNWX	CE	Berlioz
92034	EG	HX	WTAE	CE	Kipling
92035	EP	HX	WNTS	CE	Mendelssohn
92036	EG	HX	WNTR	CE	Bertolt Brecht
92037	EG	HX	WTAE	CE	Sullivan
92038	EP	ET	GBET	CO	Voltaire
92039	EG	HX	WNTS	CE	Johann Strauss
92040	EP	ET	GBET	CO	Goethe
92041	EG	HX	WNTR	CE	Vaughan Williams
92042	EG	HX	WTAE	CE	Honegger
92043	EP	ET	GBET	CO	Debussy
92044	EP	ET	GBET	CO	Couperin
92045	EP	ET	PTXX	LB (S)	Chaucer
92046	EP	ET	PTXX	LB (S)	Sweelinck

3. EUROTUNNEL LOCOMOTIVES

DIESEL LOCOMOTIVES

0001–0005   MaK   Bo-Bo

Built: 1991–1992 by MaK at Kiel, Germany (Model DE1004).
Engine: MTU 12V 396 TC13 of 940 kW (1260 h.p.) at 1800 rpm.
Main Alternator: ABB.   **Traction Motors:** ABB.
Maximum Tractive Effort: 305 kN (68600 lbf).
Continuous Tractive Effort: 140 kN (31500 lbf) at 20 mph.
Power At Rail: 750 kW (1012 h.p.). **Dimensions:** 14.40 x ?? m.
Brake Force: 120 kN.   **Wheel Diameter:** 1000 mm.
Weight: 82 t.   **Maximum Speed:** 100 km/h.
Design Speed: 120 km/h.   **Train Brakes:** Air.
Fuel Capacity: 3500 litres.   **Multiple Working:** Within class.
Train Supply: Not equipped.   **Signalling System:** TVM430 cab signalling.

Note: Registered on TOPS as 21901–905.

0001	**GY**	ET	CO
0002	**GY**	ET	CO
0003	**GY**	ET	CO
0004	**GY**	ET	CO
0005	**GY**	ET	CO

0031–0042   HUNSLET/SCHÖMA   0-4-0

Built: 1989–1990 by Hunslet Engine Company at Leeds as 900 mm gauge.
Rebuilt: 1993–1994 by Schöma in Germany to 1435 mm. gauge.
Engine: Deutz of 270 kW (200 h.p.) at ???? rpm.
Transmission: Mechanical.   **Maximum Tractive Effort:**
Cont. Tractive Effort: **Power At Rail:**
Brake Force: **Dimensions:**
Weight: **Wheel Diameter:**
Design Speed: 50 km/h.   **Maximum Speed:** 50 km/h.
Fuel Capacity: **Train Brakes:** Air.
Train Supply: Not equipped.   **Multiple Working:** Not equipped.

0031	**GY**	ET	CO	FRANCES
0032	**GY**	ET	CO	ELISABETH
0033	**GY**	ET	CO	SILKE
0034	**GY**	ET	CO	AMANDA
0035	**GY**	ET	CO	MARY
0036	**GY**	ET	CO	LAURENCE
0037	**GY**	ET	CO	LYDIE
0038	**GY**	ET	CO	JENNY
0039	**GY**	ET	CO	JILL
0040	**GY**	ET	CO	PACITA

| 0041 | **GY** | ET | CO | KIM |
| 0042 | **GY** | ET | CO | NICOLE |

ELECTRIC LOCOMOTIVES

9001–9838   BRUSH/ABB   Bo-Bo-Bo

Built: 1993–2002 by Brush Traction at Loughborough.
Supply System: 25 kV AC 50 Hz overhead.
Traction Motors: Asea Brown Boveri design. Asynchronous 3-phase motors.
Model 6FHA 7059 (as built). Model 6FHA 7059C (7000 kW rated locos).
Maximum Tractive Effort: 400kN (90 000lbf).
Continuous Rating: Class 9/0 and 9/1: 5760 kW (7725 h.p.). Class 9/7 and 9/8:
7000 kW (9387 h.p.).

Maximum Rail Power:	**Multiple Working:** TDM system.
Brake Force: 50 t.	**Dimensions:** 22.01 x 2.97 x 4.20 m.
Weight: 136 t.	**Wheel Diameter:** 1250 mm.
Design Speed: 100 m.p.h.	**Maximum Speed:** 100 m.p.h.
Train Supply: Electric.	**Train Brakes:** Air.

Class 9/0 Original build locos. Built 1993–1994.

9005	**EB**	ET	CO	JESSYE NORMAN
9007	**EB**	ET	CO	DAME JOAN SUTHERLAND
9011	**EB**	ET	CO	JOSÉ VAN DAM
9013	**EB**	ET	CO	MARIA CALLAS
9015	**EB**	ET	CO	LÖTSCHBERG 1913
9018	**EB**	ET	CO	WILHELMENA FERNANDEZ
9022	**EB**	ET	CO	DAME JANET BAKER
9024	**EB**	ET	CO	GOTTHARD 1882
9026	**EB**	ET	CO	FURKATUNNEL 1982
9029	**EB**	ET	CO	THOMAS ALLEN
9033	**EB**	ET	CO	MONTSERRAT CABALLE
9036	**EB**	ET	CO	ALAIN FONDARY
9037	**EB**	ET	CO	GABRIEL BACQUIER
9040	**EB**	ET	CO	

Class 9/1. Freight Shuttle dedicated locos. Built 1998–2001. These locos are
being refurbished and renumbered in the 9/7 series.

9105	**EB**	ET	CO
9106	**EB**	ET	CO
9108	**EB**	ET	CO
9109	**EB**	ET	CO
9110	**EB**	ET	CO
9111	**EB**	ET	CO
9112	**EB**	ET	CO
9113	**EB**	ET	CO

Class 9/7. Increased power freight shuttle locos. Built 2001–2002.

| 9701 | **EB** | ET | CO |
| 9702 | **EB** | ET | CO |

9703		**EB**	ET	CO
9704		**EB**	ET	CO
9705		**EB**	ET	CO
9706		**EB**	ET	CO
9707		**EB**	ET	CO

9711	(9101)	**EB**	ET	CO
9712	(9102)	**EB**	ET	CO
9713	(9103)	**EB**	ET	CO
9714	(9104)	**EB**	ET	CO
9715	(9105)			
9716	(9106)			
9717	(9107)	**EB**	ET	CO
9718	(9108)			
9719	(9109)			
9720	(9110)			
9721	(9111)			
9722	(9112)			
9723	(9113)			

Class 9/8 Locos rebuilt from Class 9/0 by adding 800 to the loco number. Uprated to 7000 kW.

9801	**EB**	ET	CO		LESLEY GARRETT
9802	**EB**	ET	CO		STUART BURROWS
9803	**EB**	ET	CO		BENJAMIN LUXON
9804	**EB**	ET	CO		VICTORIA DE LOS ANGELES
9806	**EB**	ET	CO		REGINE CRESPIN
9808	**EB**	ET	CO		ELISABETH SODERSTROM
9809	**EB**	ET	CO		FRANÇOIS POLLET
9810	**EB**	ET	CO		JEAN-PHILIPPE COURTIS
9812	**EB**	ET	CO		LUCIANO PAVAROTTI
9814	**EB**	ET	CO	(S)	LUCIA POPP
9816	**EB**	ET	CO		WILLARD WHITE
9817	**EB**	ET	CO	(S)	JOSÉ CARRERAS
9819	**EB**	ET	CO		MARIA EWING
9820	**EB**	ET	CO		NICOLAI GHIAUROV
9821	**EB**	ET	CO		TERESA BERGANZA
9823	**EB**	ET	CO		DAME ELISABETH LEGGE-SCHWARZKOPF
9825	**EB**	ET	CO		
9827	**EB**	ET	CO		BARBARA HENDRICKS
9828	**EB**	ET	CO		DAME KIRI TE KANAWA
9831	**EB**	ET	CO		
9832	**EB**	ET	CO		RENATA TEBALDI
9834	**EB**	ET	CO		MIRELLA FRENI
9835	**EB**	ET	CO		NICOLAI GEDDA
9838	**EB**	ET	CO		HILDEGARD BEHRENS

▲ Arriva "executive"-liveried 57314 arrives at Crewe with the 16.15 Cardiff Central–Holyhead on 05/07/10. **Cliff Beeton**

▼ Aggregate Industries-liveried 59005 "KENNITH J PAINTER" passes Reading with 7C77 12.40 Acton Yard–Merehead empty stone train on 04/06/10.
Jason Rogers

▲ 60071 "Ribblehead Viaduct" heads north at Chevin, between Duffield and Belper, with 6E38 04.57 Didcot–Lindsey empty oil tanks on 03/05/10.   **Phil Chilton**

▼ The only Class 66 in DB Schenker livery at the time of writing – 66152 – passes Swinton with 6M59 01.07 New Cumnock–Ratcliffe loaded coal on 24/03/09.
Robert Pritchard

▲ Original GBRf-liveried 66706 "Nene Valley" storms through Hatfield Peverel on 11/08/10 with 4L02 04.40 Hams Hall–Felixstowe intermodal. GBRf is now owned by Eurotunnel. **Robert Pritchard**

▼ Colas Rail-liveried 66841 passes North Stafford Junction, south of Derby, with 6Z56 06.04 Washwood Heath–Boston on 13/04/10. **Phil Chilton**

▲ EWS-liveried 67002 "Special Delivery" hauls 91122 and the diverted 10.32 Wakefield Westgate–London King's Cross (via Leeds) at Cross Gates on 24/04/10.   **Robert Pritchard**

▼ 67029 "Royal Diamond" in DBS silver livery leads 1A80 06.04 York–Kensington Olympia Northern Belle south on the ECML near Sandy on 22/06/10. 67028 was on the rear.   **John Pink**

▲ One of the new Freightliner Class 70s, 70005, leaves Stud Farm Quarry heading towards Knighton Junction, Leicester with 6Z22 14.25 Stud Farm–Crewe loaded ballast on 24/05/10. **Paul Biggs**

▲ Two-tone grey-liveried 73107 passes Putney with 1Q11 04.33 Eastleigh–Selhurst test train on 22/04/10. 31233 was on the rear. **Chris Wilson**

▼ BR Electric blue-liveried 86259 "Les Ross" passes Golborne Junction, near Wigan, with a return Vintage Trains Ravenglass–Birmingham charter on 30/05/09. **Terry Eyres**

▲ Carrying the new Freightliner green & yellow livery, 90045 passes Brantham, near Manningtree, with 4M81 07.34 Felixstowe–Ditton intermodal on 31/08/10.
Antony Guppy

▲ The first Class 91 in the new East Coast silver livery, 91107, arrives at Doncaster with the 08.30 London King's Cross–Newcastle on 11/09/10. **Marcus Fudge**

▼ In two-tone grey with Europorte brandings, Eurotunnel's 92028 is seen near Polhill with 6Z93 14.12 Willesden–Dollands Moor test working on 09/07/10.
Alex Dasi-Sutton

4. FORMER BR MAIN LINE LOCOS IN INDUSTRIAL SERVICE

Former British Rail main line locomotives considered to be in "industrial use" are listed here. These locomotives do not currently have Network Rail engineering acceptance for operation on the national railway network.

Number   Other no./name   Location

Class 11

12088		Johnson's (Chopwell), Steadsburn Disposal Point, Widdrington

Class 03

03112	D2112	Victoria Group, Port of Boston, Boston
03179	CLIVE	First Capital Connect, Hornsey Depot, London
03196	JOYCE/GLYNIS	West Coast Railway Company, Carnforth
D2381		West Coast Railway Company, Carnforth

Class 07

07001		Barrow Hill Roundhouse, Chesterfield
D2991	07007	Knights Rail Services, Eastleigh Works

Class 08

08202	CHUFFER	Gloucestershire Warwickshire Railway
08331		Midland Railway-Butterley, Derbyshire
08375		Tata Steel, Trostre Works, Llanelli, Carmarthenshire
08411		Colne Valley Railway, Essex
08417		RVEL, RTC Business Park, Derby
08418		West Coast Railway Company, Carnforth
08423	H011 14	PD Ports, Teesport, Grangetown, Middlesbrough
08441		LH Group Services, Barton-under-Needwood
08445		Tata Steel, Shotton Works, Deeside, Flintshire
08447		John G Russell (Transport), Hillington, Glasgow
08460		Felixstowe Dock & Railway Company, Felixstowe
08484	CAPTAIN NATHANIEL DARELL	Felixstowe Dock & Railway Company, Felixstowe
08485		West Coast Railway Company, Carnforth
08492		Barrow Hill Roundhouse, Chesterfield
08499		Pullman Rail, Canton Depot, Cardiff
08502	Lybert Dickinson	Northern, Heaton Depot, Newcastle
08503		Railway Support Services, Rye Farm, Wishaw, Sutton Coldfield
08507		Bombardier Transportation, Central Rivers Depot, Barton-under-Needwood
08511		Felixstowe Dock & Railway Company, Felixstowe
08517		St Modwen Properties, Long Marston
08523		Celtic Energy, Onllwyn Coal & Distribution Centre, West Glamorgan
08527		Flixborough Wharf, Flixborough, Scunthorpe

08536		RVEL, RTC Business Park, Derby
08568	St. Rollox	Railcare, Springburn Depot, Glasgow
08573		Bombardier Transportation, Ilford Works, London
08588	17	PD Ports, Teesport, Grangetown, Middlesbrough
08598	H016 HERCULES	The Potter Group, Queen Adelaide, Ely
08600		AV Dawson, Ayrton Rail Terminal, Middlesbrough
08602	004	Bombardier Transportation, Derby Works
08613	H064	Hanson Cement, Ketton Cement Works, Stamford
08622	H028 19	PD Ports, Teesport, Grangetown, Middlesbrough
08629		Railcare, Wolverton Works, Milton Keynes
08643		Hanson Aggregates, Whatley Quarry, near Frome
08648	OLD GEOFF	Wabtec Rail, Doncaster Works
08649	G.H. Stratton	Railcare, Wolverton Works, Milton Keynes
08650	ISLE OF GRAIN	Bardon Aggregates, Isle of Grain, Kent
08652		Hanson Aggregates, Whatley Quarry, near Frome
08665		Barrow Hill Roundhouse, Chesterfield
08668		St Modwen Properties, Long Marston
08670		Colne Valley Railway, Essex
08678	ARTILA	West Coast Railway Company, Carnforth
08682	Lionheart	Bombardier Transportation, Derby Works
08683		Gloucestershire Warwickshire Railway
08697		RVEL, RTC Business Park, Derby
08699		Tata Steel, Shotton Works, Deeside, Flintshire
08704	D3871	Victoria Group, Port of Boston, Boston
08730	The Caley	Railcare, Springburn Depot, Glasgow
08743	Bryan Turner	SembCorp Utilities Teesside, Wilton, Middlesbrough
08750		First Capital Connect, Hornsey Depot, London
08754		Wabtec Rail, Doncaster Works
08756		Tata Steel, Shotton Works, Deeside, Flintshire
08762		Wabtec Rail, Doncaster Works
08764	003 FLORENCE	Maritime Transport, Tilbury Railport, Tilbury
08774	ARTHUR VERNON DAWSON	AV Dawson, Ayrton Rail Terminal, Middlesbrough
08787	08296	Hanson Aggregates, Machen Quarry, near Newport
08807		AV Dawson, Ayrton Rail Terminal, Middlesbrough
08809		Tata Steel, Shotton Works, Deeside, Flintshire
08810		LNWR, Crewe Carriage Depot
08813		St Modwen Properties, Long Marston
08818	MOLLY	Flixborough Wharf, Flixborough, Scunthorpe
08823	LIBBIE	Thamesteel, Sheerness Steelworks, Isle of Sheppy
08827		St Modwen Properties, Long Marston
08834		Bombardier Transportation, Old Dalby test centre
08846	003	Bombardier Transportation, Derby Works
08868		LNWR, Crewe Carriage Depot
08870	H024	Weardale Railway, Wolsingham
08871		Wabtec Rail, Doncaster Works
08873		Freightliner, Maritime Terminal, Southampton
08881		Gloucestershire Warwickshire Railway
08885	H042 18	PD Ports, Teesport, Grangetown, Middlesbrough
08892		Lafarge, Blue Circle Cement Works, Hope, Derbyshire
08903	JOHN W. ANTILL	SembCorp Utilities Teesside, Wilton, Middlesbrough

08912		AV Dawson, Ayrton Rail Terminal, Middlesbrough
08913		Daventry International Railfreight Terminal, Crick
08928		St Modwen Properties, Long Marston
08933		Bardon Aggregates, Merehead Stone Terminal
08936		Tata Steel, Shotton Works, Deeside, Flintshire
08937	BLUEBELL MEL	Bardon Aggregates, Meldon Quarry, Okehampton
08943		Barrow Hill Roundhouse, Chesterfield
08947		Bardon Aggregates, Merehead Stone Terminal
08956		Bombardier Transportation, Old Dalby test centre

Class 09

09003	Boden Rail, Washwood Heath Depot, Birmingham
09012	Barrow Hill Roundhouse, Chesterfield
09018	Boden Rail, Washwood Heath Depot, Birmingham

Class 14

| D9504 | | Kent & East Sussex Railway |
| D9529 | 14029 | Bardon Aggregates, Bardon Hill Quarry, Coalville |

Class 20

20056	81	Tata Steel, Appleby-Frodingham Works, Scunthorpe
20066	82	Tata Steel, Appleby-Frodingham Works, Scunthorpe
20168	SIR GEORGE EARLE	Lafarge Cement, Blue Circle Cement Works, Hope, Derbyshire

Class 56

| 56009 | 56201 | Brush Traction, Loughborough Works |

Class 73

| 73119 | Borough of Eastleigh | Knights Rail Services, Eastleigh Works |

NS Class 600

This class, built by English Electric, resembles the BR Class 08s and these locos, now in industrial use in the UK, are included here for clarity (two others of this class are preserved in the UK).

625	690	H043	16	PD Ports, Teesport, Grangetown, Middlesbrough
627	685	H045		Midland Railway-Butterley, Derbyshire
632	687	H046	9	Thamesteel, Sheerness Steelworks, Isle of Sheppy
649	692	H049	13	St Modwen Properties, Long Marston
653		H050		Weardale Railway, Wolsingham

5. LOCOMOTIVES AWAITING DISPOSAL

Locomotives that are still extant but at scrapyards or considered to be awaiting disposal are listed here. It should be noted that some of the locos listed here may see further use on the main line if they are resold by scrap merchants.

Number   Livery   Location

Class 08

08320	B	European Metal Recycling, Kingsbury
08398	B	European Metal Recycling, Kingsbury
08869	G	European Metal Recycling, Kingsbury
08872	E	European Metal Recycling, Attercliffe
08884	B	European Metal Recycling, Kingsbury
08920	F	European Metal Recycling, Kingsbury
08953	DG	European Metal Recycling, Attercliffe

Class 09

09104	DG	European Metal Recycling, Hartlepool

Class 37

37672	F	TJ Thomson, Stockton
37675	F	European Metal Recycling, Kingsbury
37893	E	Ron Hull Junior, Rotherham

Class 47

47150	FL	TJ Thomson, Stockton
47289	FF	TJ Thomson, Stockton

Class 56

56085	LH	European Metal Recycling, Hartlepool
56088	E	European Metal Recycling, Hartlepool
56108	F	European Metal Recycling, Hartlepool
56111	LH	European Metal Recycling, Hartlepool
56129	F	European Metal Recycling, Hartlepool

Class 58

58019	F	European Metal Recycling, Kingsbury
58045	F	European Metal Recycling, Kingsbury

Class 87

87011	V	European Metal Recycling, Kingsbury
87018	V	European Metal Recycling, Kingsbury
87030	V	European Metal Recycling, Kingsbury
87032	V	European Metal Recycling, Kingsbury

6. LOCOMOTIVES EXPORTED FOR USE ABROAD

This section details former BR (plus privatisation era) diesel and electric locomotives that have been exported from the UK for use in industrial locations or by a main line operator abroad. Not included are locos that are "preserved" abroad, which are included in our "Preserved Locomotives" publication. Generally locos are included here if they are expected to remain abroad for more than one year. The DB Schenker Class 66s in use with DBS subsidiary Euro Cargo Rail in France are now also listed here as these only now return to Toton for major maintenance.

Number   *Other no./name*   *Location*

Class 04

D2289		Lonato SpA, Lonato Steelworks, Lonato, Brescia, Italy

Class 08

08738		Euro Cargo Rail, Vallourec pipe works, Déville-les-Rouen, France
08939		Euro Cargo Rail, Vallourec pipe works, Déville-les-Rouen, France

Class 37

37703	L25	Continental Rail, Spain
37714	L26	Continental Rail, Spain
37716	L23	Continental Rail, Spain
37718	L22	Continental Rail, Spain
37799	L27	Continental Rail, Spain (withdrawn)
37800	L33	Continental Rail, Spain
37801	L29	Continental Rail, Spain (withdrawn)
37883	L28	Continental Rail, Spain (withdrawn)
37884	L34	Continental Rail, Spain

Class 58

58001		ETF, Villersexel, France
58004		TSO, Villersexel, France
58005		ETF, Villersexel, France
58006		ETF, Villersexel, France
58007		TSO, Villersexel, France
58009		TSO, Villersexel, France
58010		TSO, Villersexel, France
58011		TSO, Villersexel, France
58013		ETF, Villersexel, France
58015	L54	Continental Rail, Spain
58018		TSO, Villersexel, France
58020	L43	Continental Rail, Spain
58021		ETF, Villersexel, France
58024	L42	Continental Rail, Spain
58025	L41	Continental Rail, Spain
58026		TSO, Villersexel, France

58027	L52	Continental Rail, Spain
58029	L44	Continental Rail, Spain
58030	L46	Continental Rail, Spain
58031	L45	Continental Rail, Spain
58032		ETF, Villersexel, France
58033		TSO, Villersexel, France
58034		TSO, Villersexel, France
58035		TSO, Villersexel, France
58036		ETF, Villersexel, France
58038		ETF, Villersexel, France
58039		ETF, Villersexel, France
58040		TSO, Villersexel, France
58041	L36	Continental Rail, Spain
58042		ETF, Villersexel, France
58043	L37	Continental Rail, Spain
58044		ETF, Villersexel, France
58046		TSO, Villersexel, France
58047	L51	Continental Rail, Spain
58049		ETF, Villersexel, France
58050	L53	Continental Rail, Spain

Class 59

59003	YEOMAN HIGHLANDER	
	259 003-2	Heavy Haul Power International, Germany

Class 66

66022	Euro Cargo Rail, France
66032	Euro Cargo Rail, France
66036	Euro Cargo Rail, France
66038	Euro Cargo Rail, France
66045	Euro Cargo Rail, France
66049	Euro Cargo Rail, France
66052	Euro Cargo Rail, France
66064	Euro Cargo Rail, France
66179	Euro Cargo Rail, France
66190	Euro Cargo Rail, France
66195	Euro Cargo Rail, France
66202	Euro Cargo Rail, France
66203	Euro Cargo Rail, France
66205	Euro Cargo Rail, France
66208	Euro Cargo Rail, France
66209	Euro Cargo Rail, France
66210	Euro Cargo Rail, France
66211	Euro Cargo Rail, France
66212	Euro Cargo Rail, France
66214	Euro Cargo Rail, France
66215	Euro Cargo Rail, France
66216	Euro Cargo Rail, France
66217	Euro Cargo Rail, France
66218	Euro Cargo Rail, France
66219	Euro Cargo Rail, France

66220		DB Schenker Rail Polska, Poland
66222		Euro Cargo Rail, France
66223		Euro Cargo Rail, France
66224		Euro Cargo Rail, France
66225		Euro Cargo Rail, France
66226		Euro Cargo Rail, France
66228		Euro Cargo Rail, France
66229		Euro Cargo Rail, France
66231		Euro Cargo Rail, France
66233		Euro Cargo Rail, France
66234		Euro Cargo Rail, France
66235		Euro Cargo Rail, France
66236		Euro Cargo Rail, France
66240		Euro Cargo Rail, France
66241		Euro Cargo Rail, France
66242		Euro Cargo Rail, France
66244		Euro Cargo Rail, France
66245		Euro Cargo Rail, France
66246		Euro Cargo Rail, France
66247		Euro Cargo Rail, France
66582	66009	Freightliner, Poland
66583	66010	Freightliner, Poland
66584	66011	Freightliner, Poland
66586	66008	Freightliner, Poland
66624	66102	Freightliner, Poland
66625	66101	Freightliner, Poland

Class 86

86232	0450 003-3	FLOYD, Hungary
86248	0450 001-7	FLOYD, Hungary
86250	0450 002-5	FLOYD, Hungary

Class 87

87003	87003-0	BZK, Bulgaria
87004	87004-8 Britannia	BZK, Bulgaria
87006	87006-3	BZK, Bulgaria
87007	87007-1	BZK, Bulgaria
87008	87008-9	BZK, Bulgaria
87010	87010-5	BZK, Bulgaria
87012	87012-1	BZK, Bulgaria
87013	87013-9	BZK, Bulgaria
87014	87014-7	BZK, Bulgaria
87019	87019-6	BZK, Bulgaria
87020	87020-4	BZK, Bulgaria
87022	87022-0	BZK, Bulgaria
87026	87026-1	BZK, Bulgaria
87028	87028-7	BZK, Bulgaria
87029	87029-5	BZK, Bulgaria
87033	87033-7	BZK, Bulgaria
87034	87034-5	BZK, Bulgaria

7. CODES

7.1. LIVERY CODES

Livery codes are used to denote the various liveries carried. It is impossible to list every livery variation which currently exists. In particular items ignored for this publication include:

- Minor colour variations.
- Omission of logos.
- All numbering, lettering and brandings.

Descriptions quoted are thus a general guide only. Logos as appropriate for each livery are normally deemed to be carried.

The colour of the lower half of the bodyside is stated first. Minor variations to these liveries are ignored.

Code	Description
1	"One" (metallic grey with a broad black bodyside stripe. White National Express "interim" stripe as branding).
AB	Arriva Trains Wales "executive" dark & light blue.
AI	Aggregate Industries (green, light grey & blue).
AL	Advertising/promotional livery (see class heading for details).
AR	Anglia Railways (turquoise blue with a white stripe).
AZ	Advenza Freight (deep blue with green Advenza brandings).
B	BR blue.
BA	British American Railway Services (dark green).
BL	BR Revised blue with yellow cabs, grey roof, large numbers & logo.
CD	Cotswold Rail (silver with blue & red logo).
CE	BR Civil Engineers (yellow & grey with black cab doors & window surrounds).
CS	Colas Rail (yellow, orange & black).
CU	Corus (silver with red logos).
DB	DB Schenker (Deutsche Bahn red with grey roof and solebar).
DG	BR Departmental (dark grey with black cab doors & window surrounds).
DR	Direct Rail Services (dark blue with light blue or dark grey roof).
DS	Revised Direct Rail Services (dark blue, light blue & green. "Compass" logo).
E	English Welsh & Scottish Railway (maroon bodyside & roof with a broad gold bodyside band).
EB	Eurotunnel (two-tone grey with a broad blue stripe).
EC	East Coast (silver with a purple stripe).
EG	"EWS grey" (as F but with large yellow & red EWS logo).
EL	Electric Traction Limited (silver & red).
EP	European Passenger Services (two-tone grey with dark blue roof).
F	BR Trainload Freight (two-tone grey with black cab doors & window surrounds. Various logos).
FA	Fastline Freight (grey & black with white & orange stripes).

FB	First Group dark blue.
FE	Railfreight Distribution International (two tone-grey with black cab doors & dark blue roof).
FER	Fertis (light grey with a dark grey roof & solebar).
FF	Freightliner grey (two-tone grey with black cab doors & window surrounds. Freightliner logo).
FH	Revised Freightliner {PowerHaul} (dark green with yellow ends & a grey stripe/buffer beam).
FL	Freightliner (dark green with yellow cabs).
FO	BR Railfreight (grey bodysides, yellow cabs & red lower bodyside stripe, large BR logo).
FR	Fragonset Railways (black with silver roof & a red bodyside band lined out in white).
FS	First Group (indigo blue with pink & white stripes).
FY	Foster Yeoman (blue & silver. Cast numberplates).
G	BR Green (plain green, with white stripe on main line locomotives).
GB	GB Railfreight (blue with orange cantrail & solebar stripes, orange cabs).
GC	Grand Central (all over black with an orange stripe).
GG	BR green (two-tone green).
GL	First Great Western locos (green with a gold stripe (no gold stripe on shunters)).
GN	Great North Eastern Railway {modified} (dark blue with white National Express "interim" stripe as branding).
GS	Royal Scotsman/Great Scottish & Western Railway (maroon).
GV	Gatwick Express EMU (red, white & indigo blue with mauve & blue doors).
GW	Great Western Railway (green, lined out in black & orange).
GX	Gatwick Express InterCity (dark grey/white/burgundy/white).
GY	Eurotunnel (grey & yellow).
HA	Hanson Quarry Products (dark blue/silver with oxide red roof).
IC	BR InterCity (dark grey/white/red/white).
K	Black.
LH	BR Loadhaul (black with orange cabsides).
LM	London Midland (white/grey & green with broad black stripe around the windows).
M	BR maroon.
MA	Maintrain/East Midlands Trains blue.
ML	BR Mainline Freight (aircraft blue with a silver stripe).
MM	Old Midland Mainline (teal green with grey lower bodyside & three tangerine stripes).
MN	Midland Mainline (thin tangerine stripe on the lower bodyside, ocean blue, grey & white).
MT	GB Railfreight Metronet (blue with orange cabsides).
N	BR Network South East (white & blue with red lower bodyside stripe, grey solebar & cab ends).
NX	National Express (white with grey ends).
O	Non-standard livery (see class heading for details).
RG	BR Parcels (dark grey & red).
RP	Royal Train (claret, lined out in red & black).
RT	RT Rail (black, lined out in red).
RV	Riviera Trains (Oxford blue).

RX	Rail Express Systems (dark grey & red with or without blue markings).
RZ	Royal Train revised (plain claret, no lining).
SD	South West Trains outer suburban {Class 450 style} (deep blue, orange & red).
SL	Silverlink (indigo blue with white stripe, green lower body & yellow doors).
ST	Stagecoach {long-distance stock} (white & dark blue with dark blue window surrounds and red & orange swishes at unit ends).
TT	Transmart Trains (all over green).
U	Plain white or grey undercoat.
V	Virgin Trains (red with black doors extending into bodysides, three white lower bodyside stripes).
VP	Virgin Trains shunters (black with a large black & white chequered flag on the bodyside).
VT	Virgin Trains silver (silver with red roof. Red swept down at ends).
WA	Wabtec Rail (black).
WC	West Coast Railway Company maroon (57601 carries a black bodyside stripe).
WS	Wrexham & Shropshire (two-tone grey & silver).
XC	CrossCountry (two-tone silver with deep crimson ends and pink doors).
Y	Network Rail yellow.

7.2. OWNER CODES

Locomotives and rolling stock are owned by various companies and private owners and are allotted codes as follows:

Code	Owner
20	Class 20189
40	The Class 40 Preservation Society
47	The Stratford 47 Group
50	Class 50 Alliance
70	7029 Clun Castle
2L	Class 20 Locomotive Society
A	Angel Trains
AI	Aggregate Industries
AM	Alstom
BA	British American Railway Services
BN	Beacon Rail
CS	Colas Rail
DB	DB Schenker Rail (UK) / DB Regio UK
DR	Direct Rail Services
DT	The Diesel Traction Group
E	Eversholt Rail (UK)
EL	Electric Traction Limited
EM	East Midlands Trains
EP	Europhoenix
ET	Eurotunnel
EU	Eurostar (UK)

FA Fastline (*in administration*)
FG First Group
FL Freightliner
GB GB Railfreight
HA The Hanson Group
HJ Howard Johnston Engineering
HN Harry Needle Railroad Company
HX Halifax Bank of Scotland
LM London Midland
LR Les Ross
LY Lloyds TSB
MW Martin Walker
NM National Museum of Science & Industry
NR Network Rail
NS Nemesis Rail
NY North Yorkshire Moors Railway Enterprises
P   Porterbrook Leasing Company
PO Other owner
PU Pullman Rail
RE Railway Vehicle Engineering
RL RMS Locotec
RV Riviera Trains
SF SNCF (Société Nationale des Chemins de fer Français)
SN Southern
TT Transmart Trains
WA Wabtec Rail
WC West Coast Railway Company
X   Sold for scrap/further use and awaiting collection or owner unknown.

7.3. LOCOMOTIVE POOL CODES

Locomotives are split into operational groups ("pools") for diagramming and maintenance purposes. The official codes used to denote these pools are shown in this publication.

Code   *Pool*

ACAC Electric Traction Limited locomotives
ACXX Electric Traction Limited locomotives for static depot use.
ADFL Advenza Freight locomotives (stored).
ATLO Alstom Class 08.
ATZZ Alstom locomotives for disposal.
CFOL Class 50 Operations locomotives.
COLO Colas Rail locomotives.
DFGC Freightliner Intermodal Class 86/5.
DFGH Freightliner Heavy Haul Class 70.
DFGI Freightliner Intermodal Class 70.
DFGM Freightliner Intermodal Class 66.
DFHG Freightliner Heavy Haul modified Class 66 (general).
DFHH Freightliner Heavy Haul Class 66.
DFIM Freightliner Intermodal modified Class 66.

DFIN	Freightliner Intermodal Class 66 (low emission).
DFLC	Freightliner Intermodal Class 90.
DFLH	Freightliner Heavy Haul Class 47.
DFLS	Freightliner Class 08.
DFNC	Freightliner Intermodal Class 86/6.
DFNR	Freightliner Heavy Haul modified Class 66. Infrastructure services.
DFRT	Freightliner Heavy Haul Class 66. Infrastructure services.
DFTZ	Freightliner stored Class 66.
DHLT	Freightliner locomotives awaiting maintenance/repair/disposal.
EFOO	First Great Western Class 57.
EFPC	First Great Western Class 43.
EFSH	First Great Western Class 08.
EHPC	CrossCountry Class 43.
EJLO	London Midland Class 08.
ELRD	East Lancashire Railway-based main line registered locomotives.
EMPC	East Midlands Trains Class 43.
EMSL	East Midlands Trains Class 08.
EPXX	Europhoenix Class 86.
ETLO	Electric Traction Limited locomotives.
GBCM	GB Railfreight Class 66. General.
GBED	GB Railfreight Class 73.
GBEE	GB Railfreight Class 20. On hire from GB Railfreight for London Underground stock moves.
GBET	Europorte2 Class 92.
GBMU	GB Railfreight Class 66. Modified for rolling stock movements.
GBRT	GB Railfreight Class 66. Porterbrook spot-hire locos.
GBSD	GB Railfreight Class 66. RETB fitted.
GBZZ	GB Railfreight. Stored locomotives.
GCHP	Grand Central Class 43.
GPSS	Eurostar (UK) Class 08.
HBSH	Wabtec hire shunting locomotives.
HNRL	Harry Needle Railroad Company hire locomotives.
HNRS	Harry Needle Railroad Company stored locomotives.
HTLX	Hanson Traction locomotives.
HWSU	Southern Class 09.
HYWD	South West Trains Class 73.
IANA	National Express East Anglia Class 90.
IECA	East Coast Class 91.
IECP	East Coast Class 43.
IVGA	Southern Class 73 (standby use).
IWCA	Virgin Trains Class 57.
MBDL	Non TOC-owned diesel locomotives.
MBED	Non TOC-owned electro-diesel locomotives.
MBEL	Non TOC-owned electric locomotives.
MOLO	Class 20s for London Underground rolling stock moves.
MRSO	RMS Locotec Class 08.
NRLO	Nemesis Rail locomotives.
PTXX	Europorte2 stored locomotives.
QACL	Network Rail Class 86.
QADD	Network Rail diesel locomotives.
QCAR	Network Rail New Measurement Train Class 43.

QETS	Network Rail Class 37.
QSTR	Network Rail stored locomotives.
RCJZ	Fastline stored locomotives.
RFSH	Wabtec Rail locomotives.
RTLO	Riviera Trains operational fleet.
RVLO	Rail Vehicle Engineering/British American Railway Services locomotives.
SAXL	Eversholt Rail (UK) off-lease locomotives.
SBXL	Porterbrook Leasing Company off-lease locomotives.
WAAN	DB Schenker Network Class 67.
WABN	DB Schenker Network Class 67. RETB fitted.
WAFN	DB Schenker Network Class 67 for hire to First Great Western.
WAWN	DB Schenker Network Class 67 for hire to Wrexham & Shropshire.
WBAI	DB Schenker Industrial Class 66.
WBAK	DB Schenker Construction Class 66.
WBAM	DB Schenker Energy Class 66.
WBAN	DB Schenker Network Class 66.
WRBI	DB Schenker Industrial Class 66. RETB fitted.
WBBK	DB Schenker Construction Class 66. RETB fitted.
WBBN	DB Schenker Network Class 66. RETB fitted.
WBES	DB Schenker Class 66. Sandite pool (locos returned from Euro Cargo Rail, France).
WBLI	DB Schenker Industrial Class 66. Dedicated locos for Lickey Incline banking duties.
WBST	DB Schenker Class 66. Sandite pool (fitted with trip cocks).
WBSN	DB Schenker Class 66. Sandite pool (general).
WCAI	DB Schenker Industrial Class 60.
WCAK	DB Schenker Construction Class 60.
WCAM	DB Schenker Energy Class 60.
WCAN	DB Schenker Network Class 60.
WCBI	DB Schenker Industrial Class 60. Extended-range fuel tanks.
WCBK	DB Schenker Construction Class 60. Extended-range fuel tanks.
WCBM	DB Schenker Energy Class 60. Extended-range fuel tanks.
WCBN	DB Schenker Network Class 60. Extended-range fuel tanks.
WDAI	DB Schenker Industrial Class 59.
WDAK	DB Schenker Construction Class 59.
WEFE	DB Schenker Network Class 90.
WFMS	DB Schenker Fleet Management Unit locomotives (Sandite cover).
WFMU	DB Schenker Fleet Management Unit locomotives.
WNTR	DB Schenker locomotives – tactical reserve.
WNTS	DB Schenker locomotives – tactical stored unserviceable.
WNWX	DB Schenker main line locomotives – for major repairs.
WNXX	DB Schenker locomotives – stored.
WNYX	DB Schenker locomotives – Fleet Management Unit (standby).
WSSI	DB Schenker Industrial operational Shunters.
WSSK	DB Schenker Construction operational Shunters.
WSSN	DB Schenker Network operational Shunters.
WSXX	DB Schenker shunting locomotives – internal/depot us
WTAE	DB Schenker Network Class 92.
WZTS	DB Schenker locomotives – tactical stored.
XHAC	Direct Rail Services Class 47.
XHCK	Direct Rail Services Class 57.

XHHP	Direct Rail Services locomotives – holding pool.	
XHIM	Direct Rail Services locomotives – Intermodal traffic.	
XHNC	Direct Rail Services locomotives – nuclear traffic/general.	
XHSS	Direct Rail Services stored locomotives.	
XYPA	Mendip Rail Class 59/1.	
XYPO	Mendip Rail Class 59/0.	

7.4. ALLOCATION & LOCATION CODES

Allocation codes are used in this publication to denote the normal maintenance base ("depots") of each operational locomotive. However, maintenance may be carried out at other locations and may also be carried out by mobile maintenance teams.

Location codes are used to denote common storage locations whilst the full place name is used for other locations. The designation (S) denotes stored. However, when a loco pool code denotes that a loco is stored anyway, then the (S) is not shown.

Code	*Location*	*Depot Operator*
BA	Crewe Basford Hall Yard	*Storage location only*
BH	Barrow Hill (Chesterfield)	Barrow Hill Engine Shed Society
BI	Brighton Lovers Walk	Southern
BK	Bristol Barton Hill	DB Schenker Rail (UK)
BN	Bounds Green (London)	East Coast
BQ	Bury (Greater Manchester)	East Lancashire Rly/Riley & Son Railways
BS	Bescot (Walsall)	DB Schenker Rail (UK)
BZ	St Blazey (Par)	DB Schenker Rail (UK)
CD	Crewe Diesel (*closed*)	DB Schenker Rail (UK)
CE	Crewe International	DB Schenker Rail (UK)
CO	Coquelles (France)	Eurotunnel
CP	Crewe Carriage	LNWR (part of Arriva)
CQ	Crewe (The Railway Age)	LNWR Heritage Company
CR	Crewe Gresty Lane	Direct Rail Services
CS	Carnforth	West Coast Railway Company
DC*	Didcot Yard	DB Schenker Rail (UK)
DR	Doncaster	DB Schenker Rail (UK)
DY	Derby Etches Park	East Midlands Trains
EC	Edinburgh Craigentinny	East Coast
EH	Eastleigh	DB Schenker Rail (UK)
FD	Freightliner diesels nationwide	Freightliner
FE	Freightliner electrics nationwide	Freightliner
GL	Gloucester Horton Road	*Storage location only*
HP*	Hope Cement Works	Lafarge
HT	Heaton (Newcastle)	Northern
IM	Immingham	DB Schenker Rail (UK)
	Inverness	ScotRail
LA	Carlisle Kingmoor	Direct Rail Services
LB	...minster	Severn Valley Railway Company
	...outh)	First Great Western
	...Works	Brush Traction

Code	Location	Operator
LD	Leeds Midland Road	Freightliner
LE	Landore (Swansea)	First Great Western
LH*	LH Group, Barton-under-Needwood	LH Group Services
LL	Edge Hill (Liverpool)	Alstom
LM	Long Marston (Warwickshire)	Motorail Logistics
MA	Manchester Longsight	Alstom
MD	Merehead	Mendip Rail
MG	Margam (Port Talbot)	DB Schenker Rail (UK)
MH	Millerhill (Edinburgh)	DB Schenker Rail (UK)
NC	Norwich Crown Point	National Express East Anglia
NL	Neville Hill (Leeds)	East Midlands Trains/Northern
NY	Grosmont (North Yorkshire)	North Yorkshire Moors Railway Enterprises
OD*	Old Dalby test centre	Bombardier Transportation UK
OO	Old Oak Common HST	First Great Western
OY	Oxley (Wolverhampton)	Alstom
PM	St. Philip's Marsh (Bristol)	First Great Western
PZ	Penzance Long Rock	First Great Western
SE	St Leonards (Hastings)	St Leonards Railway Engineering
SL	Stewarts Lane (London)	Southern/VSOE
SK	Swanwick Junction (Derbyshire)	Midland Railway-Butterley
SO	Soho (Birmingham)	London Midland
SP	Springs Branch (Wigan)	DB Schenker Rail (UK)
SU	Selhurst (Croydon)	Southern
SZ	Southampton Maritime	Freightliner
TE	Thornaby (Middlesbrough)	DB Schenker Rail (UK)
TI	Temple Mills (London)	Eurostar (UK)
TM	Tyseley Locomotive Works	Birmingham Railway Museum
TO	Toton (Nottinghamshire)	DB Schenker Rail (UK)
TS	Tyseley (Birmingham)	London Midland
TY	Tyne Yard (Newcastle)	DB Schenker Rail (UK)
WA	Warrington	DB Schenker Rail (UK)
WB	Wembley (London)	Alstom
WD	Wimbledon (London)	South West Trains
WF	Wansford (Cambridgeshire)	Nene Valley Railway
WH*	Washwood Heath (Birmingham)	Boden Rail Engineering
WN	Willesden (London)	London Overground
WO*	Wolsingham, Weardale Railway	British American Railway Services
YK	National Railway Museum (York)	National Museum of Science & Industry
ZA	RTC Business Park (Derby)	Railway Vehicle Engineering
ZB	Doncaster Works	Wabtec Rail
ZC	Crewe Works	Bombardier Transportation UK
ZD	Derby Works	Bombardier Transportation UK
ZG	Eastleigh Works	Knights Rail Services
ZH	Springburn Depot (Glasgow)	Railcare
ZI	Ilford Works	Bombardier Transportation UK
ZJ	Stoke Works	Axiom Rail (Stoke)
ZK	Kilmarnock Works	Brush-Barclay
ZN	Wolverton Works	Railcare
ZR	York (Holgate Works)	Network Rail

*= unofficial code.